Chocolate Fortunes

The Battle for the Hearts, Minds, and Wallets of China's Consumers

Lawrence L. Allen

Foreword by Dr. Ángel Cabrera, President,
Thunderbird School of Global Management

American Management Association

New York • Atlanta • Brussels • Chicago • Mexico City • San Francisco
Shanghai • Tokyo • Toronto • Washington, D.C.

Special discounts on bulk quantities of AMACOM books are available to corporations, professional associations, and other organizations. For details, contact Special Sales Department, AMACOM, a division of American Management Association, 1601 Broadway, New York, NY 10019.
Tel.: 800-250-5308 Fax: 518-891-2372
E-mail: specialsls@amanet.org
Website: www.amacombooks.org/go/specialsales
To view all AMACOM titles go to: www.amacombooks.org

This publication is designed to provide accurate and authoritative information in regard to the subject matter covered. It is sold with the understanding that the publisher is not engaged in rendering legal, accounting, or other professional service. If legal advice or other expert assistance is required, the services of a competent professional person should be sought.

Although this book does not always specifically identify trademarked terms, AMACOM uses them for editorial purposes only, with no intention of trademark violation. A list of trademarked terms used in this book appears on page viii.

Library of Congress Cataloging-in-Publication Data

Allen, Lawrence L., 1960–
    Chocolate fortunes : the battle for the hearts, minds, and wallets of China's consumers / Lawrence L. Allen.
        p.   cm.
    Includes index.
    ISBN-13: 978-0-8144-1432-3 (hardcover)
    ISBN-10: 0-8144-1432-X (hardcover)
    1. Chocolate industry—China—History.   2. Chocolate candy—China.
I. Title.
    HD9200.C42A45   2010
    338.4'7663920951—dc22

                                                           2009015464

Printing number

10   9   8   7   6   5   4   3   2   1

This book is dedicated to my parents, Louis and Kaleope Allen, whose 1980 trip to China inspired me to find my career path, and whose love and devotion to their children is the foundation of all that is good and meaningful in my life.

Contents

Chapter 6

Mars: A Well-Regulated Militia   176

Chapter 7

Going the Distance: China's 10K Chocolate Race   201

Trademarked terms in *Chocolate Fortunes:*

Almond Roca
Baby Ruth
Blue Riband
BreathSavers
Butterfinger
Cadbury Creme Eggs
Cadbury Dairy Milk
Cadbury Dairy Milk Fruit and Nut
Cadbury Roses
Cadbury Dairy Milk Whole Nut
Cailler
Carnation
Certs
Cheerios
Chunky
CoffeeMate
Coke
Crackle
Crispy Delicious Rice
Dannon
Dentyne
Doublemint
Dove
Dove Bar
Dove Promises
Dovebar ice cream
Dr. Pepper
Dreyer's
Éclairs
Ethel M
Ferrero Rocher
Future Cola
Halls
Hershey's
Hershey's Bar with Almonds
Hershey's Kisses
Hershey's Kisses with Almonds
Hershey's Nuggets
Hershey's Peanut Caramel Bar
Hershey's Special Dark
Hershey's Symphony
Hershey's Syrup
Ice Breakers
Jindi
Jinsha
Jolly Rancher
Kentucky Fried Chicken
KitKat

Kjeldsens Butter Cookies
Konabar
Lindt
M&Ms
Mar-O-Bar
Mars Bar
McDonald's
Mercedes-Benz
Milk Tray
Milky Way
Mr. Goodbar
Nescafé
Nescafé "1 + 2 sachet pack"
Nestlé Cailler Table Bomb
Nestlé Celebration
Nestlé China Crunch
Nestlé Crunch
Nestlé Infant Food
Nestlé Milk Wafer
Nestlé Wafer
Nutella
Oh Henry!
Oreo
Oreo Chocolate Wafer
PayDay
Pepsi
Perrier
Perugina's Baci Chocolate
Purina Friskies
QueQiao
Raider bar
Red October
Reese's NutRageous
Reese's Peanut Butter Cups
Ritter Sport
Schweppes
Smarties
Snapple
Snickers
Stouffer's
Sugus
Taster's Choice
3 Musketeers
TicTac
Twix
Uncle Ben's
Whac-a-Mole
White Rabbit

Foreword

Cacao began its global journey over five hundred years ago when the Spanish conquistadors brought seeds back to Spain from Mesoamerica and introduced what would become an icon of the Western world's decadence and indulgence to Europe. Only during the last quarter of a century has cacao's journey extended into China.

Today, world business leaders are captivated by the sheer size of the China market, and those in the global chocolate industry are no exception. In *Chocolate Fortunes*, Lawrence Allen, a Thunderbird alumnus, paints a compelling, comprehensive, and dynamic portrait of the global chocolate industry's quarter-of-a-century endeavor to capture the mindshare and taste buds of Chinese consumers, which proved a Sisyphean challenge for most.

It is fitting that this story be told by a Thunderbird alumnus. For the last sixty-two years, Thunderbird has been dedicated to educating global leaders who can break barriers, build bridges of cooperation and understanding, and create new ventures that bring about prosperity around the world. Thunderbird's approach is a combination of global mind-set (an appreciation of cultural and institutional differences), global entrepreneurship (turning differences into opportunities to create value), global connections (the ability to build trusting and productive relationships across boundaries), and global citizenship (a commitment to creating sustainable value for all parties involved in a global business enterprise). Allen's career is the ultimate Thunderbird story. And he uses it to thoughtfully extract lessons that can be of great value to many other leaders involved in the fascinating world of global business.

Allen skillfully weaves the story of the evolution of the Chinese economy from austerity to increasing affluence since it opened to the West just over thirty years ago. While he does this through the lens of the chocolate industry in China, the tapestry of *Chocolate Fortunes* is a rich story of evolving social, cultural, and economic Chinese dynamics and how these interact with the business drama that focuses on one industry's major global competitors. Allen's ability to shift back and forth between the specific practices and mind-sets of competitors in the chocolate industry and the Chinese context in which they compete is engaging, entertaining, and informative.

Chocolate Fortunes is a complex story representative of almost all industries that have entered this market, considered one of the most challenging in the world. Allen's firsthand account of the five global chocolate titans—Ferrero, Cadbury, Hershey, Nestlé, and Mars—documents five market entry approaches and the impact of each competitor's administrative heritage that led each to take the path it chose. As important, Allen documents the impact that leaders' decisions have on a company's success. His in-depth description of common China challenges such as local copycats, logistics nightmares, culturally based challenges, and the emergence of credible local competitors provides generalizable lessons for any company considering entry into the increasingly sophisticated China market.

China and the China market provided a perfect laboratory in which different market entry "experiments" could play out. The evolution of the Chinese economy has been spectacular and much faster than anticipated. Most early China scholars and business investors cannot believe the pace and scope of change in thirty years. The chocolate industry is an understandable one—and one that generates considerable passion and strong preferences among consumers. The chocolate industry competitors encountered a clean slate in China, and this gave each a perfect opportunity to shape the consumer's reality in its favor. Allen's combination of this location in this time frame for this industry provides a remarkable panoramic comparison for marketers, strategists, and leaders alike. It is rare that such a comprehensive story can be documented and presented in such a compelling fashion. This story could only have been told by a perceptive person with a front-row seat and hands-on experience with the steps and missteps of the chocolate industry in this most recent leg of its journey and the fits and starts of China's recent economic and social evolution.

Dr. Ángel Cabrera
Professor and President
Thunderbird School of Global Management

Dr. Mary Teagarden
Professor of Global Business
Thunderbird School of Global Management
Editor of the *Thunderbird International Business Review*

Acknowledgments

I would like to thank all those who contributed to the creation of *Chocolate Fortunes*, starting with my literary agent Katherine Boyle, who was the first person to express interest in a book about chocolate and China; my editor at AMACOM, Bob Nirkind, who shared that interest; and Peter Zheutlin, who, together with Bob, profoundly influenced the crafting of this book. My thanks as well to Jeffrey Eugenides for his sage advice about the mysterious world of publishing, and to my friends and colleagues who generously shared their experiences and insights: Li Jianmin, Andrew Lau, Derek Lai, Beiye, Linda Yang, Yew-Kong Kok, Danny Xu, John Zhang, Roger Luo, David Wan, and all those not mentioned here. A special thanks to Joyce Ni, waitress at the Beijing Capital Paradise clubhouse restaurant, who always provided service with a smile and kept the coffee flowing late into the evening during the writing of this book.

Introduction
One Country, Three Centuries

China's breathtaking transformation from a command to a market-socialist economy over the past twenty-five years has turned some 300 million of its 1.3 billion people into ravenous consumers of everything from candy to cars. And until twenty-five years ago, almost none of them had ever eaten a piece of chocolate. They were, to coin a phrase, "chocolate virgins," their taste for chocolate ready to be shaped by whichever chocolate company came roaring into the country with a winning combination of quality, marketing savvy, and manufacturing and distribution acumen. In short, China was the next great frontier, a market of almost limitless potential to be conquered in a war between the world's leading chocolate companies for the hearts, minds, and taste buds—and ultimately the wallets—of China's consumers. To the victor of the chocolate wars would go the spoils of over a billion potential customers for generations to come.

Despite China's radical transformation over the past quarter century, from economic basket case to economic powerhouse, it is still a work in progress. Figuratively speaking, in China today there are fewer than 50 million people living in the twenty-first century, about 300 million living in various stages of the twentieth century, and nearly a billion people living in the latter part of the nineteenth century. Nevertheless, China's economic renaissance over the past two and a half decades has been nothing short of astonishing, especially considering the havoc wreaked by the failed economic, social, and cultural experiments of the 1950s, 1960s, and 1970s—and the brutality with which they were carried out. This period would, however, prove to be the dark hour before the dawn of China's emergence, under Deng Xiaoping,[1] into the global economy, a process begun in the late 1970s.

And while China's transformation is unprecedented, so too was the establishment of foreign businesses within a major country undergoing a complete economic and social transformation from a centrally planned economy to a market-socialist economy.

* * * * *

For seven years, between 1998 and 2006, I was a foot soldier in the "chocolate war," first as an executive with Hershey, and later Nestlé, two of the world's largest manufacturers of chocolate; as such, I was on the front lines of a battle for the hearts, minds, and taste buds of more than a quarter billion people constituting China's new consumer class.

This book is the story of the five global titans of chocolate—Ferrero, Cadbury, Hershey, Nestlé, and Mars—that battled to capture a once-in-a-lifetime opportunity to establish their brands with one-fifth of the world's population. It is also the inside story of East meeting West through the introduction into China, a xenophobic land of austerity and deprivation, of an icon of the Western world's decadence and self-indulgence: chocolate.

When I first arrived in China in the 1980s, I was a newly minted MBA; a twenty-something, "me-generation" American looking for adventure and riches in this vast economic frontier. The country was then in the early, experimental phase of its social and economic transformation, and trying to do business there meant wading endlessly through the detritus of vestigial government organs and policies while attempting to find purchase on its ever-changing economic and regulatory landscape. A high tolerance for ambiguity was essential.

Two early experiences exemplify the Alice in Wonderland nature of doing business there at the time, and it is a tale of two cities: Beijing, the belly of China's centrally planned communist beast; and Shenzhen, the tip of the spear of China's economic reforms.

During my final semester of graduate school at the Thunderbird School of Global Management, I co-founded Transnational Trade Services, a general trading company with glamorous headquarters in my Arizona dorm room. My most promising client was an American antiques buyer, and shortly after graduation I traveled to China together with my classmate and Chinese business partner, Li Jianmin, to find a source for Chinese antiques.

Upon arriving in Beijing we went to meet a former associate of Li's, a branch manager of a state-owned trading company, to see whether he could help us locate and export antiques. His office was located in an unimpressive, soot-covered one-story government building; it was not exactly an auspicious beginning, and our fortunes didn't improve from there. Though we were greeted politely, through Li's trustworthy translation and my basic Mandarin Chinese, it quickly became clear that this gentleman was a midlevel, lifelong bureaucrat comfortably ensconced in a large bureaucracy. As we talked, I became increasingly mindful of the portrait of Chairman Mao,[2] literally and figuratively looking over his shoulder. Throughout our discussion he was consistently oblique and noncommittal.

The business we were proposing would be new to him and his department, he said, and would require approvals from many different people in many different agencies. This would be difficult and would take time. Finding the antiques we were looking for would also be a time-consuming process, and even with the approvals and the goods in hand, export procedures would be cumbersome. Where we saw opportunity he saw barriers. Perhaps, we thought, we would make more progress over a meal, and we invited our host to lunch. By the time we left the building for a nearby restaurant, we had nearly a dozen of his colleagues in tow. It seemed he'd invited nearly everyone in his office. Far too much food and too many bottles of wine were ordered, and when we parted my lunch guests were loaded down with doggie bags full of food and wine, a bounty they would share with grateful families that evening.

As I reflected on what had gone wrong, I realized that, for many in China, it must be difficult and risky to break with old habits. This gentleman had nothing to gain from meeting with us—other than a free lunch with enough left over for his family. If something went wrong, he would have a problem on his hands. If he did nothing, he would still get his government pay, housing, and benefits. Why take a chance? I clearly had a lot to learn about doing business in China.

Shortly after this encounter, as a tourist accompanying a Taiwan tour group, I took a trip to Hong Kong, then a British colony. After several days of shopping and sightseeing, we boarded a bus for a day trip across the border to Shenzhen, one of the special economic development zones created by China in the 1980s as an early experiment in capitalism. As we approached the border, the travel agent running the tour handed each passenger a stack of documents and five hundred Hong Kong dollars (about US$65)—everyone except me, that is. When I asked why I'd been overlooked, one of my fellow passengers explained that the government was trying to encourage ethnic Chinese from Taiwan, Hong Kong, and Macau to come to mainland China to aid in the development of their ancestral homeland. As an incentive, first-time arrivals, even if just visitors, were allowed to bring motorcycles, refrigerators, and a host of other high-value consumer goods into the country duty-free. These goods would be ready and waiting on the Hong Kong side of the border and the stack of papers being distributed on the bus were for customs. The travel agent offered qualified passengers that money to carry the documents through Chinese customs, where they would then receive the necessary "chop" (application of an official government seal). The goods listed on the forms didn't belong to the passengers; the passengers were simply being "encouraged" to act as document mules for the travel agent, who would collect the chopped documents on the Chinese side of the border and send them to business associates in Hong Kong. Those documents would then be used to bring merchandise into China duty-free. In essence, it was a scheme that parlayed the duty-exempt status of Taiwan, Hong Kong, and Macau Chinese visiting the country into a lucrative, multimillion-dollar, duty-free import business.

This experience couldn't have been more different from the one I had recently had in Beijing. Shenzhen was a whirlwind of frenzied and unbridled Wild West–style capitalism. Beijing, on the other hand, appeared stuck in a time warp of monolithic central planning and ossified bureaucracy. This perplexing dichotomy raised the question: What is the right way to do business in China? It is a question I have been trying to answer ever since, for China today remains both of these places. There are no simple answers in China—just endless questions, as the Big Five chocolate companies that battled for dominance in China would find out.

* * * * *

Perhaps the best known, but most misunderstood expression to come out of China's transformational era is a simple but powerful statement made by China's Paramount Leader, Deng Xiaoping: "It doesn't matter if a cat is black or white, so long as it catches mice." In its most elementary form, this was a straightforward philosophical statement in support of economic pragmatism. Some Western pundits mistook the statement as a swipe at communism and China's one-party system, suggesting that democracy and full-scale capitalism were just around the corner. They were not. Deng Xiaoping was an ardent communist to the end of his life. Though he made the statement in 1961, from 1978 onward the black cat/white cat metaphor would have great symbolic meaning among the

Chinese as a challenge to decades of a self-destructive, obsessive fascination with the concept of class struggle as a means to building an egalitarian society. In retrospect, it also signaled the turn from a ruinous era of economic and social chaos driven by rigid ideological orthodoxy to a transformational era of unprecedented economic growth and prosperity—one that continues to this day.

In 1978, of course, the path to this growth and prosperity was unclear and the challenge staggering. But what was clear to Deng and his fellow reformists was that the time for endless debates about economic theory had come to an end, and the time to unlock the energy, strength, ingenuity, creativity, and adaptability of the Chinese people had arrived. As Deng said of the transformation that lay ahead: "We must cross the river by feeling the stones with our feet."

China's transition to world economic powerhouse would take thirty years, and the development of its chocolate market was inexorably tied to the various stages of this remarkable social and economic transformation. For the world's leading chocolate companies, China was a new frontier with boundless possibility, and indeed, even today the potential for growth is breathtaking. But the chocolate war wasn't simply a fight for the hearts, minds, and taste buds of Chinese consumers, nor was it simply a battle among the chocolate companies involved. It was also a struggle for global chocolate companies to discern a route to commercial success in China.

Each player came to the battlefield equipped with its own arsenal of strengths. Italian chocolate maker Ferrero, the Ferrari of chocolate, had Ferrero Rocher, a unique product—a delicate chocolate and hazelnut confection encased in an elegant gold foil wrapper—and an upscale cachet that had a proven appeal to chocolate consumers worldwide. Cadbury was the chocolate of the British Empire and had a presence in Britain's Chinese enclaves during the colonial era. Hershey, the purveyor of the great American chocolate bar, had a less-than-stellar track record in the international arena but brought a much-needed will to find a way in China. Nestlé, the Swiss-based global food titan, and by some reckoning the world's largest seller of chocolate, brought enormous resources and extensive experience to global markets. Mars, an American family-owned chocolate giant, had a reputation as a tough street fighter and a determination to succeed in the China market.

The battle for China's chocolate market holds lessons for anyone doing, or about to do, business in this most dynamic of markets. There is no single path to business success there, however; the country is too big, too complex, and evolving too quickly for simple, "one size fits all" business formulas. Nevertheless, the story of the chocolate war is highly instructional.

But the story of the opening of China's chocolate market isn't simply a business story; it's a window into the world's most populous country—one that is, almost by the day, acquiring greater and greater economic and political clout and positioning itself for a powerful, if not preeminent role, in shaping world events and the global future. Never before has China's destiny been so closely intertwined with our own, or with the rest of the world's. And for years, never had the future of chocolate been so intertwined with one nation's perilous transformation from rags to riches.

CHAPTER 1

China and Chocolate

East Meets West

A famous colonial-era saying from the mid-1800s held that if Chinese men added just an inch to the length of their shirttails, fortunes would flow to English textile mills. Such overreaching ambitions have been typical of foreign companies that have eyed the China market for centuries.

The reality for British colonial-era merchants was that their wares rarely reached beyond the small foreign enclaves scattered along China's coast. Most Chinese, however, were physically, and culturally, beyond the coast. They had their own clothing fashions and styles, for example, and except perhaps for the few who regularly mixed with foreigners, they weren't much interested in English textiles, which were far too expensive for nearly all Chinese anyway. In short, the vast majority of the population was inaccessible: physically, culturally, and financially.

More than a century later, the same is true about the nearly 1 billion Chinese (of a total population of 1.3 billion) who still live, figuratively speaking, in the nineteenth century; they are simply out of reach for most foreign companies. Even if the Big Five chocolate companies were able to get their products in front of these consumers, chocolate is so foreign that it would have limited appeal to their untrained palates. And who would spend almost a day's wages on a chocolate bar? Thus, the battle for China's chocolate affections has been limited to its emerging consumer class in the major cities.

China is one of humankind's oldest civilizations, perhaps the oldest civilization in continuous existence, ruled by a virtually unbroken series of successive imperial dynasties that stretches back thousands of years. Its break with its imperial lineage occurred so recently that even as late as the 1990s it wasn't uncommon to see little old ladies shuffling along Chinese streets on bound feet, a practice that faded only with the end of the Qing Dynasty, China's last imperial dynasty, in 1911.[1] One could even read an interview with a Qing Dynasty–era eunuch in a Chinese newspaper just a decade ago.

China has its own complex and illustrious history, with a cultural DNA that evolved from Confucian[2] philosophy and that developed independently from Judeo-Christian societies in the West. The cultural crevasse between China and the West reaches down to the most fundamental cultural values, and one of those cultural values is food itself. Judeo-Christian cultures have evolved on the principle that "man does not live by bread alone," meaning that physical nourishment is only a part of life and implying that satisfying spiritual needs is also essential. Chinese, on the other hand, have viewed food as *min yi shi wei tian*, "for people, food is heaven,"[3] meaning that the essence of what is most important in life is a full belly. Though this view has become somewhat of a quaint cultural vestige among the most prosperous and worldly of China's modern-day big-city dwellers, for the vast majority of people, the country's rural poor in particular, it is a belief that is still very much alive and all too relevant to their daily lives. A good example of this can be found in the way many people still greet each other in China: *"chi fan le mei you,"* ("Have you eaten?"). Big Five chocolate company executives needed to grasp the significance of these kinds of fundamental cultural differences to formulate successful plans for introducing their products to Chinese consumers in a way that was meaningful to them. And some of the more influential differences between China and the outside world resulted more from its recent history than from its ancient cultural characteristics.

China's recent isolation from the outside world and economic debacles that occurred during the 1950s, 1960s, and 1970s ensured that all of the Big Five chocolate companies shared the same anonymity with China's consumers. Furthermore, since chocolate had no history or tradition in China, to speak of, it was a completely foreign product to virtually all Chinese when it arrived in the 1980s. Each of the Big Five chocolate companies—Ferrero, Cadbury, Hershey, Nestlé, and Mars—would make a contribution to the development of China's chocolate market, simply by establishing a presence there. However, the one that could establish a culinary and cultural bridge between its products and China's emerging consumers, successfully navigate the complexities and ambiguities of China's rapidly transforming economic system, and best understand consumers' common experience through their country's recent history would be the one to establish its chocolate as the preferred chocolate taste among China's first generation of chocolate consumers and could declare victory in China's chocolate war.

China's Road from Communism to Market Socialism

When Deng Xiaoping deftly managed his gradual rise to power to become the de facto leader of the People's Republic of China in 1978,[4] and began advancing his agenda of economic pragmatism, he had both the opportunity and the challenge of rebuilding his country's economy. By then, the Chinese people had suffered decades of war, economic setbacks, and stagnation. After thirteen years of war during the 1930s and 1940s[5] that cost over 20 million lives, and a respite of relative stability during much of the 1950s, the country was plunged into three successive calamities that would leave an indelible mark on Chinese society for generations.

The first of these calamities was the Great Leap Forward (1958–1960), an attempt by Mao Zedong to accelerate modernization of both China's industry and agriculture simultaneously, with a single five-year government economic plan. This involved the government's taking total control of and microadministrating both economic sectors. The fundamental approach was to reassemble society into communes, and then make each commune self-sufficient in everything from steel manufacturing to food production. However, this monumental effort was fraught with confusion, mismanagement, and inefficiency. China's industries produced little of usable value, and the imposition of radical and unproven farming techniques caused agricultural production to plummet. The final result was to force people to squander what little they had on outlandish economic and social experiments.

This debacle was followed by the Great Chinese Famine (1958–1961). The wholesale experimentation with China's industry and agriculture during the Great Leap Forward, compounded by unfavorable weather patterns, eventually took its toll on the Chinese economy and people, culminating in what some reckon to have been one of the largest famines in human history. Estimates of total deaths by starvation vary widely, but it was most certainly somewhere within the range of official Chinese government estimates of 15 million and independent estimates of 40 million people during this three-year period.

The final calamity was the Great Cultural Revolution (1966–1976). In 1966, through his media apparatus, and under the guise of saving the communist revolution, Mao called upon China's youth to abandon their schools and their families, and band together into so-called Red Guard brigades to carry on the revolutionary class struggle. Numbering in the tens of millions, and with only the teachings of Mao's *Little Red Book* and other political propaganda to guide them, individual bands of Red Guards transformed themselves into a barbarous menagerie that terrorized the population, all done in the service of Mao's vision of a rigid communist state under his singular authority. At its peak, it resulted in nationwide social and cultural vandalism,[6] and it was a period of unprecedented fear, violence, and suffering.

At the end of the 1970s, China emerged upon the world scene a broken country. Its agricultural sector was in a shambles, and while a state-owned industrial sector existed, it was for the most part antiquated and plagued by poor management, low-quality goods, and low productivity. China's Communist Party–controlled, centrally planned economy was a disaster, and it would take decades to develop a viable commercial law system and overcome the isolation that allowed few Chinese to even imagine any kind of life beyond their daily subsistence–level existence. The task ahead for Deng Xiaoping and his reformers was daunting, to say the least.

Deng's first initiative, known as the Four Modernizations Policy, focused on bringing the industrial, agricultural, scientific, and military sectors of the economy into the twentieth century. However, with the breakup of the Soviet Union still more than a decade away, there was no roadmap for transitioning an economy based on Communist Party dogma to the kind of market-socialist economy Deng envisioned. China would be the first. Though Deng was a visionary, even he most likely could not have envisioned the China we know today.

Although China's modern transformation began in 1978, it unfolded in three phases over three decades. From the perspective of the Big Five chocolate companies, these phases could fairly be called the "experimental phase" of the 1980s, the "critical-mass phase" of the 1990s, and the "break-away phase," which started around 2000 and continues to this day.

The experimental phase was marked by bureaucratic complexity, regulatory ambiguity, and a general state of confusion

that, although worlds better than the draconian era that preceded it, presented significant difficulties when doing business in China. The country's infrastructure was antiquated
and poorly maintained. It was so difficult and time-consuming to make a domestic phone call, for example, that many
offices employed full-time phone dialers, who often spent half
an hour or more to get a single call through. Even seemingly
simple activities such as sending a truckload of merchandise
from the north to the south of the country required several
cross-dockings[7] at provincial borders along the way, since few
trucks had license plates that worked across all of the country's provinces and drivers needed to obtain travel permits to
move between provinces.

The pervasive confusion of the experimental phase was
partly attributable to inexperience with market systems and,
as a result of the social chaos of the Cultural Revolution, the
rule of law. New policies and regulations promulgated almost
daily exacerbated the situation, both for foreigners doing
business in China and for the Chinese themselves, and there
was a sense among many people there that there were no stable guidelines or limits. In spite of these difficulties, business
was conducted, most successfully, between Hong Kong and
the southern Chinese provinces. This was a golden era for
Hong Kong because the modern-day silk road[8] for imported
goods bound for China ran through Hong Kong. As Deng's
economic reforms began to take effect during the 1980s, and
factories sprung up to meet the country's growing export demand, people began to get money in their pockets, and they
wanted to spend it on imported consumer goods. The pent-up
demand was so great that virtually any product brought into
China was immediately sold, albeit in relatively small quanti-

ties. Throughout the experimental phase, consumer-product companies enjoyed a success born of curiosity simply by making their products available.

It took more than a decade of cumulative political and economic reform, infrastructure development, and foreign investment to finally achieve the chain reaction, or critical mass, in China's economy that enabled its economic engine to begin running more smoothly, rather than in sputters and misfires. Materials and resources that were once difficult to find were readily available, power supply to factories was more steady and reliable, office space could be found in major cities and foreign-invested companies no longer needed to operate out of hotel rooms, air transportation between major cities was more dependable and routine, and basic commercial mechanisms were finally in place. During this critical-mass phase, the focus in the business community turned from what couldn't be done to what could now be done. For foreign consumer-product companies it was the beginning of the era of real competition in the China market, since market conditions had reached the point where they were able to take an active interest in the marketing and distribution of their products there. And this meant in-country marketing, sales, and distribution management.

Companies that had simply been exporting *to* China set up shop *in* China to be better positioned to seize opportunities in the country's rapidly emerging consumer market. And once there, the foreign companies and their products enjoyed great prestige and credibility among the populace, whether deserved or not. The challenges, however, were considerable. Building a business in China meant hiring employees (both expats and locals) and developing effective cross-cultural business organizations. The first major challenge was finding the right leaders for their China organizations. Few companies at the time had an internal bench of management talent that had practical experience in China. Most companies, therefore, faced an either/or proposition: either send an employee who knew the company and the business but didn't know China, or hire someone who knew China but didn't know the company and the business. It was the single most important decision that the Big Five chocolate companies would need to make, since their China business leaders, and the continuity and quality of leadership that the companies were able to sustain over time, had a profound impact on the ultimate outcome of China's Chocolate War.

When hiring Chinese employees, the Big Five ran into another major challenge that would require a significant and sustained commitment from the companies to bring their China organizations up to speed. The devastating impact of the Cultural Revolution on China's education system,[9] combined with only a rudimentary knowledge of modern business practices, meant that there was an extremely limited domestic talent pool, particularly in business administration, finance, marketing, and sales. Foreign business executives and technicians, whom the Chinese referred to as foreign experts, were expected to be oracles for every aspect of their business and operations. Prospective employees would often show up for interviews at foreign companies with only basic English-language skills and a lot of enthusiasm. Therefore, to accomplish its goal of economic transformation, China needed to undertake a fifth modernization—education—in addition to its official Four Modernizations. Foreign-invested companies obliged by investing a significant amount of time and effort in training their Chinese employees, not only through on-the-job training and internal training programs but also through tuition reimbursement for MBA programs and even overseas developmental assignments for high-potential employees. As a result, the influx of foreign companies during the 1990s rapidly accelerated this knowledge transfer and over the decade helped create China's first generation of ambitious, educated, and experienced employees, who have become key to its remarkable economic success.

But perhaps the most important catalyst for accelerating the growth of consumer-product businesses, chocolate in particular, was the development of suitable retail environments, which began during the critical-mass phase. By the mid-1990s, vast numbers of kiosks and neighborhood markets had sprouted up across the country. Although the number of quality retail environments in all of China—those with air-conditioning, such as hypermarkets (superstores) and high-end supermarkets—was in the hundreds, and there were perhaps a few thousand convenience stores, all located predominantly in large cities such as Beijing, Shanghai, and Guangzhou, these quality retail outlets became the gateway for making chocolate accessible to Chinese consumers.

The current phase of China's transformational era, the break-away phase, can be exemplified through numerous examples. For instance, whereas in the 1980s a simple phone call required businesses to employ phone dialers, now there are more than 400 million cell phones in use throughout the country (100 million more cell phones than there are people in the United States). Also, the thirty-year exclusive reign of the expatriate business manager is quickly drawing to a close, as highly qualified and now experienced Chinese executives assume leadership roles in multinational companies where they are better suited to keep pace with the country's rapidly changing market dynamics and emerging opportunities, and to lead China's economic growth, innovation, and change. And by 2007, China's economy had grown to be the world's fourth largest, just behind Germany.[10]

But this phase is more importantly about a new mind-set and changing perceptions about China's place in the world than it is about any particular economic achievement or analysts' statistical hurdles. The world has substantially altered its traditional perception of the country as nothing more than a supplier of cheap exports. Indeed, with China's economic growth having accounted for 27 percent of total global economic growth in 2007,[11] its economy has become the world's industrial growth engine and is now viewed as an indispensable component of the global economy.

This break-away phase is a tectonic shift in the mind-set of the Chinese people and how they view themselves and their nation's place in the world. This can be found in a new self-confidence and pride that is evident in, and reinforced by, events such as Beijing's successful hosting of the 2008 Summer Olympics, putting a person into space (one of only three nations to do so), and in the commercial arena, the purchase by Lenovo, a Chinese company, of IBM's PC business, just to name a few. The Chinese have broken away from the self-perception of being a poor and disadvantaged nation victimized by a century of war, political turmoil, and economic privation, and after decades of feeling like second-class citizens, they are ascendant on the world scene.

The Evolution of the Global Chocolate Industry

Chocolate is made from the seeds of the cacao tree, which is native to South America, has been under cultivation there for thousands of years, and was prepared as a beverage. The Spaniards in the mid-1500s brought it back to Europe, where it became a popular exotic drink among European royalty and aristocrats. By the mid-1700s it had become more commonplace, served as a beverage in European chocolate houses. Solid forms of chocolate for eating first appeared in Europe around the same time, but it would take another century of experimentation and development for drinking chocolate to evolve into the edible milk chocolate we know today.[12] Milk chocolate is made by first separating two ingredients from the cocoa bean: cocoa butter and cocoa powder. They are then reconstituted and mixed in varying proportions with milk (condensed milk or powdered milk, depending on the process) and sugar. Chocolate quality is principally defined by three factors: particle size, conch (mixing) time, and cocoa butter content. The smaller the particle size, the more smooth and creamy the feeling is in the mouth. The longer the conch time, the more developed the flavor becomes. And since cocoa butter melts at just below body temperature, the more cocoa butter a chocolate has, the more it delivers that satisfying melty feeling in the mouth. Cocoa butter also coats the mouth and taste buds, which results in chocolate's pleasant lingering aftertaste.

From a luxurious beverage of European high society to its ubiquitous "grab-n-go" presence next to virtually every cash register today, chocolate, whether boxed for Valentine's Day, molded into chocolate bunnies for Easter, or packaged in red and green foil for Christmas, has become integral to the Western world's cuisine and lifestyle.

The companies that continue to dominate the chocolate industry today are the same ones that founded the industry over the last century. Three of the Big Five chocolate companies—Cadbury, Hershey, and Nestlé—all began making milk chocolate at more or less the same time, during the last two decades of the nineteenth century. Mars was a relative latecomer, incorporating in 1911 as the Mar-O-Bar Company, and arriving on the chocolate scene with its popular Milky Way bar in 1923. Ferrero was the last, incorporating in the late 1940s and launching its Ferrero Rocher chocolate in 1982. With just six companies accounting for 80 percent[13] of the world's retail chocolate[14] market, it is an old and established industry, with powerhouse products and brands that have stood the test of time, some for over a century.

One reason the Big Five have been able to hold on to their dominance is that the industrial process for mass-producing high-quality chocolate is capital intensive, and the delicate and highly complex production process is not easily replicated or mastered. The main reason for this longevity is consumers' unusually strong loyalty to the taste of their chocolate; many consumers make a lifetime commitment to their favorite chocolate brands. Therefore, even only slight variations in a chocolate's taste or texture are detectable by regular chocolate consumers. For example, one Australian chocolate lover, whose favorite was Cadbury Dairy Milk Chocolate, went without eating chocolate during a two-week business trip to England because she didn't like the taste of British-made Cadbury chocolate. On subsequent trips to England,

Cadbury's home country, she would take large bars of Australian-made Cadbury milk chocolate. This kind of taste loyalty is common among chocolate lovers, and combined with consumers' emotional attachment to their chocolate (people generally aren't as passionate about, say, pretzels or chewing gum), once the Big Five chocolate companies had established their products' taste across multiple generations of consumers, it became very difficult for potential competitors to make inroads. For the Big Five chocolate companies, the lack of brand awareness and established taste preferences in China was a golden opportunity to establish theirs as the preferred chocolate for hundreds of millions of potential consumers. However, in addition to China's economic and infrastructural challenges, China's vastly different culture and traditions would put the marketing skills of chocolate company executives to the test.

Chinese and Chocolate: A Foreign and Exotic Curiosity

Over the millennia, the Chinese have developed a wide variety of cuisines and an astonishingly diverse menu of food items. The successful introduction of chocolate to China faced numerous hurdles—culinary and cultural, demographic, economic, societal, logistical, and infrastructural—and understanding Chinese cuisine was a vital first step for chocolate company executives to find an entry point for chocolate in the diets of Chinese consumers.

The predominant ethnic group in China are the Han Chinese, who constitute 92 percent of the country's population,

with the remaining 8 percent accounted for by fifty-five different ethnic minorities. While China's ethnic composition is
fairly homogeneous, its culinary traditions are not. Taste preferences vary widely throughout its twenty-two provinces, but
generally speaking salty is the preferred taste in the northern
provinces; sweet and "fresh," considered a flavor in China, are
preferred in the south; spicy is favored in the central (Sichuan) and eastern provinces; and sour is favored in the
west.[15] While it is likely that chocolate consumption across
China has been influenced by these taste preferences and their
influence on Chinese cuisine, the low overall penetration of
chocolate makes it difficult to discern any particular pattern.

Ironically, in spite of such a wide variety of tastes and textures, chocolate was so foreign to the Chinese palate that the
only culinary gateway into the diets of Chinese consumers
was as a foreign and exotic curiosity. Therefore, to make their
chocolates appealing to Chinese consumers, the Big Five's
marketing approaches and products had to be consistent with
this prevailing view. This would become an advantage for
them, as Chinese companies simply did not have the foreign
credentials to make significant inroads with consumers as
credible chocolate makers. Consequently, they would remain
largely on the fringes of the retail chocolate market, presenting little if any threat to the dominance of the Big Five.

An important feature of Chinese culture that affected the
introduction of chocolate is the belief in the Yin and Yang—
the division of the natural world into two opposing but com-
plementary forces. This belief extends to food through
Chinese pharmacognosy, an ancient form of pharmacology
that calls for consumption of plants and animals in their natural unaltered forms, and that asserts that health can be main-

tained by balancing Yin and Yang forces within the body. Yin is described as the body's being in a "cool" condition, and Yang, the "heat" state, both of which can be regulated by the kinds of foods consumed. Being out of balance is considered toxic, resulting in various conditions and afflictions. For example, the body is said to have excessive Yin during the common cold, menstruation, and pregnancy, and foods thought to increase Yin, such as melons and asparagus, as well as cold drinks, are to be avoided. To restore balance, foods that bring more Yang, or "heat," into the body, such as lamb, pepper, and chocolate,[16] are recommended. Conversely, people afflicted with acne, skin rashes, allergies, and hypertension are thought to have excessive Yang and are counseled to avoid consuming Yang foods and to consume more Yin foods.[17] Whether these beliefs are scientifically sound was irrelevant insofar as the chocolate companies were concerned. The vast majority of Chinese believe it and the question, therefore, was how it would affect the way they consumed chocolate. The principal impact was that people dramatically reduced their chocolate consumption during the summer months, believing that "heaty" foods like chocolate should not be consumed when the weather was hot.[18] Consequently, chocolate company executives planned their business operations around significantly lower sales volume in summer.[19]

* * * * *

Imported chocolate was considered a luxury for the Chinese people when it first arrived in the early 1980s, and the expense was more easily justified when chocolate was given as a gift than when it was bought for self-consumption. Gift giving, therefore, became the cultural gateway for chocolate's initial entry into China, and chocolate gifts from abroad had a decisive influence on how the Chinese established their initial impression of it. The expectation was that chocolate should be imported (or at least have a foreign brand); be expensive; and, most important, deliver on the promise of a highly indulgent eating experience.

Though there are some variations, gift-giving traditions are fairly universal throughout China. Gift giving plays an important role as a social facilitator within the society, especially in business, where it is an important way to personalize business relationships and to enhance acquaintances with professional associates. In the business context, Chinese gift-giving traditions are fairly complex and chiefly governed by the so-called face factor. For example, there is a traditional gift exchange at both the start of major business negotiations and at the close of the deal. Great pains are taken to ensure that the correct gift is given for the right occasion, lest the giver or receiver lose face. The stakes are raised when gifts are given to people of higher social ranking or influence. In addition, businesses are expected to give gifts to local public officials during festivals and other special occasions to help lubricate the wheels of commerce.

Chinese gift-giving rituals, steeped in tradition and superstition, are not readily understood by foreigners, and navigating these waters can be treacherous. For example, the gift of a clock for a birthday would be a major faux pas because it implies *song zhong*, which can be translated as "send the end." To the Chinese, this is more akin to wishing someone a happy funeral than a happy birthday. It is, therefore, wise for foreigners to always seek trusted local advice when selecting a gift in China.

For most established chocolate markets around the world, chocolate for gift-giving purposes accounts for less than 10 percent of total sales, with purchases for self-consumption accounting for the rest. By contrast, in China during the 1980s and early 1990s, chocolate for gift giving accounted for well over half its sales, particularly during holiday seasons. Chocolate became a symbol of prosperity and fashionable good taste for the giver, and the more ornate and premium looking the gift's packaging, the better. In no time, chocolate took its place alongside expensive Chinese wines, cartons of imported cigarettes, and high-quality tea as favored gifts.

But a chocolate gift business does not, on its own, constitute a complete chocolate market, and the potential of chocolate in China would not be fully realized until people began purchasing chocolate for self-consumption in significant volumes. Chocolate gift sales do not require the purchaser to have a taste for chocolate—only that he or she be willing to pay the price. Chocolate sales for self-consumption would take much longer to develop, since a new generation of consumers would need to emerge, one that was more open to foreign tastes.

* * * * *

During China's decades of austerity from the 1950s through the 1970s, people had become accustomed to a limited range of foods that were predominantly indigenous. Their diets consisted of rice or noodles as a grain, some vegetables and tofu, with a little meat, poultry, or fish as a garnish. Variety was not only limited, it was also highly seasonal. Even well into the 1980s, for example, shortly after the annual harvest, Beijing was awash with cabbage. Virtually every rooftop, alley, courtyard, and doorway was stacked high with cabbages, and it wasn't difficult to guess what was on the menu for breakfast, lunch, and dinner every day for months. Older people accustomed to such a diet found the taste, texture, and particularly the sweetness of chocolate too foreign and too extreme. Consequently, as disposable incomes grew and an increasingly wider variety of foods became available during the latter 1980s and early 1990s, it was young people—those whose tastes were not shaped by decades of limited food choices—who developed broader palates at an earlier age and ultimately became the primary target market. And it was during the 1990s, when these emerging consumers began to earn more pocket money in China's rapidly growing economy, that self-consumption of chocolate began to make significant headway.

While it is difficult to imagine a society with no brothers and sisters, no cousins, and even no aunts and uncles, within the next two generations China will become the only country in the world populated predominantly by people from single-child households. The country's one-child-per-family policy, begun in the late 1970s, was a drastic effort to control its population growth, and for the most part it has succeeded.[20] The result is China's so-called 4-2-1 Society: four grandparents and two parents doting on one precious child, commonly referred to as "little emperors." Over 100 million strong,[21] demanding and wielding sufficient "pester power" to control a fair share of the combined spending power of six adults, these young consumers have a taste for Western fast foods and snacks and have become an economic force of their own. They are the first generation of Chinese consumers to grow up eating chocolate from a very early age, and they will likely lead chocolate consumption patterns to mirror those of developed chocolate markets within the space of their lifetimes. The chocolate company that wins the hearts, minds, and taste buds of these little emperors will be assured a loyal consumer base in China for decades to come.

The Size of China's Chocolate Prize

Even today, the amount of chocolate sold in China is relatively tiny. A nation of more than a billion people, it consumes about 146 million pounds (66.5 million kilograms) of chocolate annually, or 1.8 ounces (50 grams) per person. Switzerland, with a population of *less than 8 million*, consumes 167 million pounds (76 million kilograms) annually, or 22 pounds (10 kilograms) per person. Americans, by comparison, consume approximately 3 billion pounds (1.4 billion kilograms) a year, or 11.7 pounds (5.3 kilograms) per person. But per capita consumption figures don't really tell the story, because most Chinese can't find chocolate in their vicinity even if they are willing to buy it. When sizing up the opportunity in China, the key for the Big Five was identifying "geographically accessible" consumers—those to whom the product could be marketed and sold with relative ease. Defined this way, China wasn't a market of over a billion, but something far smaller: at most, 100 million in the 1980s, 200 million in the 1990s, and 300 million after 2000—or roughly the population of the

United States. But even this grossly overstated the potential, since the vast majority of Chinese consumers with access to chocolate were not likely consumers, because of either their age, their resistance to foreign foods, or their level of disposable income. Thus, despite the population size of China's geographically accessible areas, the likely market for chocolate was probably only 10 to 20 million through the 1980s, 20 to 60 million throughout the 1990s, and is only about 100 million today, roughly 8 percent of China's population. Among this smaller group, per capita consumption is still low by international standards: about 1.5 pounds (700 grams) per person, or one-eighth the average American's consumption.[22]

The difficulty in estimating something as basic as China's market size was symptomatic of one of the greatest challenges faced by business managers operating in it: the lack of basic business information. Import statistics were available from the government and provided a baseline for the amount of chocolate entering China, but as some of the Big Five began producing chocolate there, this figure became less useful. Though the government published chocolate sales estimates that showed the market growing at about 15 to 20 percent per year, these figures did not provide important detail, such as where and when it was sold, in which type of retail store, and whether the chocolate was purchased for gift giving or self-consumption—the type of data that Big Five executives had at their fingertips in their home markets from sources such as ACNielsen's Scantrack.[23] Without mechanisms in place for gathering such data in China, executives had to find other means to acquire information to help them fine-tune their sales, marketing, and distribution plans.

Quantifying China's chocolate market through projections

based on population statistics was dubious in any event, because there was no guarantee that sales in Shanghai, for instance, would be comparable to sales in Chongqing, a city with a similar population. The differences between the two cities in terms of income levels, number of air-conditioned stores, and familiarity with foreign products meant that sales in Chongqing would be far below those of Shanghai. Commercial conditions across China were simply too varied to derive accurate estimates by counting heads, and business executives were more likely to be misled by their estimates than accurately informed. With good data hard to find, innovative chocolate company executives looked to China's retail stores, which proved the best source of quantitative information about the chocolate market. A simple but effective method is to count the number of retail stores where chocolate can be sold within a particular geographic area, develop sales estimates for those stores (by assigning someone to stand in a few representative stores for a day or two to tally the number of consumer purchases),[24] and use the estimates to project a reasonable market size within that area. For all these efforts to estimate the size of the market, the one constant has been a market growth rate of between 15 and 20 percent per year; yet the important thing for the Big Five, which intended to dominate China's chocolate market, would be to well exceed this growth rate.

Today, much has changed in China's retail stores and many of them provide scanner data that can be subscribed to. Indeed, Wal-Mart, which is an important retailer in China, provides its weekly category sales data to manufacturers regularly. However, when the Big Five's executives arrived in the late 1980s and early 1990s, they faced a primitive retail environment, and the ability to improvise, adapt, and function on a more intuitive level was something they needed to quickly master. If companies sought to overanalyze the market, they risked becoming paralyzed by their own analyses and China's rapidly evolving consumer markets would pass them by before they could fully execute their plans.

Selling Chocolate

Chocolate is not a necessity and is purchased mainly to satisfy emotional needs that are fulfilled by its soothing and self-indulgent pleasures. It is generally accepted within the industry that approximately 70 percent of chocolate is purchased by consumers on impulse, and that individual branding and packaging designs for different chocolate products, even those made by the same company, are essential in driving impulse purchases. To successfully capitalize on impulse-purchase behavior, packaging must make an immediate and distinctive impression. If consumers have to carefully examine a package to make sure they are getting what they want, the impulse will often pass. Once consumers adopt a favorite chocolate product, the packaging itself can trigger the craving that leads to an impulse purchase. The sales axiom is simple: "I see, therefore I buy." A corollary of this axiom is that the more opportunities there are to catch the buyer's attention and trigger his or her craving, the higher the sales. This is why one can see the same candy on sale in dozens of locations within the same shopping mall or area; in the supermarket; or next to the cash register in the stationery store, the drugstore, the video store, the gas station, and even the office supply store.

In supermarkets, the chocolate aisle is the anchor of any chocolate company's in-store merchandising strategy. It is where the full breadth of its product range is available to consumers in a single location. But just having chocolate available in a store does not guarantee good sales. It has to be visible as well. Industry studies have shown that only 22 percent of shoppers who enter a supermarket ever walk down the chocolate aisle. That means that if a chocolate company has its products only in the chocolate aisle, nearly 78 percent of shoppers will never even see those products, and that is why chocolate companies go to great expense to get their products in every possible location within supermarkets, especially the ends of retail shelves facing main traffic aisles that feed directly into checkout lanes. And, of course, the displays within consumers' reach right near the register are critical opportunities for snaring impulse purchases.[25] These locations are known as hot spots and are consequently hotly contested locations for impulse products like chocolate.

In developed economies, a science has developed around maximizing retail sales through mastering the modern retail environment, mainly by effectively applying the three fundamental retailing principles of making products available, visible, and within reach of consumers. But when foreign consumer-product companies first began making their products available in China during the 1980s, they faced a retail infrastructure to which this science was not readily adapted. Indeed, for the first ten years of China's economic transformation, simply making their products available to Chinese consumers would present a daunting challenge for the Big Five chocolate companies.

Selling Chocolate in China

As communism permeated China during the 1950s, its entire commercial system converted from a supply-and-demand market-driven system to a centrally planned command economy. Private property was eliminated and all commercial enterprises were put under state ownership and control. From the 1950s through the end of the 1970s, privately owned retail stores, and even street peddlers, were virtually nonexistent, as they were banned by the state. During the Cultural Revolution, anyone who violated this ban risked the ire of Red Guards—the radical youth brigades who would beat them on the spot, brand them as counterrevolutionaries, and have them imprisoned.

As Deng Xiaoping's reforms began to take hold in the early 1980s, China's only retail environments were state owned, and imported luxuries such as chocolate could be found only in places such as China's Friendship Stores—big-city establishments that catered to foreign guests and the privileged or well connected. Generally dark and dingy places, they were laid out like a department store, and there were no opportunities to apply impulse-purchase merchandising techniques because almost all goods were either behind the counter or under glass, and even simple purchases were a multistep process involving considerable paperwork and the coordinated effort of several store employees. Only the most determined chocolate addict would go to all the trouble required to purchase a chocolate bar.

Food stores for the masses throughout the 1980s were, for the most part, open-air wet markets, so-called because they came complete with tubs and tanks filled with live fish, crustaceans, and sea invertebrates, in addition to baskets of fruits and vegetables, fly-encrusted bloody chopping blocks, and baskets full of rice and other grains that were weighed and bagged on the spot by attendants. Chocolate simply did not fit into the merchandising scheme of China's wet markets.

There were a small number of food stores that sold sweets and candies in behind-the-counter bulk bins, with attendants who would scoop, bag, and weigh them the way traditional candy stores used to do in the United States half a century earlier. Some foreign chocolates eventually found their way into these bulk bins toward the end of the 1980s, but again, the stores and their layout were not impulse-purchase merchandising friendly.

During this time there was almost nothing the Big Five could do to influence the distribution and merchandising of their products in China's bleak retail environment. They were left with few options but to sell their products to traders and importers at the country's border and let whatever system there was for getting their products in front of consumers do the job. In addition, China's retail environment would need to cover a century of evolution before modern-day merchandising techniques could be applied.

Remarkably, China obliged. Its retail sector leapfrogged decades of development in roughly fifteen years. By the early 1990s, small privately owned neighborhood kiosks and mom-and-pop stores began to appear throughout the country. Though large in number, they presented only a limited opportunity for chocolate, owing to its relatively high price and the stores' lack of air-conditioning. Modern-trade retail stores (air-conditioned hypermarkets or superstores, supermarkets, and convenience stores) began to emerge in the mid-1990s, and it was only then that the Big Five started making headway in applying impulse-purchase merchandising techniques in retail stores to make their products more visible and within the reach of consumers.

Though China's retail environment developed rapidly, it did not occur evenly throughout the country, and this became one of the more complex aspects of its evolving retail sector: managing a national business within China's one-country/three-centuries economy. To keep things manageable, companies segregated China into tiers defined by geography (cities); level of consumers' disposable income and exposure to foreign products; and, most important, availability of modern-trade retail stores. Cities such as Shanghai, Beijing, and Guangzhou are typical of what came to be known as first-tier cities—those with the highest level of economic development and the highest standards of living. By the late 1990s, these cities had enough accessible consumers and sufficiently developed retail and distribution infrastructures to support a substantial and robust year-round chocolate business, albeit a highly seasonal one.

Second-tier cities were more numerous but were at levels of economic development that provided fewer accessible consumers and far fewer suitable retail outlets. Third-tier cities were where, for the most part, the air-conditioned supply chain ended, and where conditions supported only a seasonal chocolate business.[26] And since the near billion Chinese consumers who lived beyond third-tier city standards were physically, culturally, and financially inaccessible for chocolate, they generally did not figure into the plans of chocolate company executives.

* * * * *

The issue of an air-conditioned supply chain was a major one for the Big Five as they formulated their China strategies. Chocolate requires storage and transportation temperatures in the range from above freezing to 61 degrees Fahrenheit (16 degrees Celsius) to maintain its consistency and surface quality. In developed markets, the so-called chilled distribution channel, or "cool channel," is an unbroken air-conditioned chain from factory to warehouse to truck to retail store. The system is so well managed that chocolate company business executives take it for granted and rarely give it a second thought. In China, however, it would become a major preoccupation.

When importing chocolate to China, the chocolate companies' problems began the moment the shipping container landed on the dock. Bureaucracy and frequent shortages of suitable delivery trucks during the 1980s and early 1990s often meant containers would sit for days or sometimes weeks at the port. Even during the late 1990s in first-tier cities, chocolate was subject to a supply chain of make-do solutions that put the product at constant risk of being heat damaged. One could observe a band of workers on a warm day unloading a truck containing cases of chocolate, bucket-brigade style, up fire escape stairs into a second-floor apartment with a window air-conditioner and newspapers taped to the windows to block the sun. From such makeshift warehouses, distributors would pick up and deliver stock to retailers using small non-air-conditioned minivans, the backseats and trunks of cars, tricycle carts, and even bicycles. Once in stores, cost-conscious retailers would turn the air conditioner on only during the day, for the comfort of themselves and their customers, and turn it off at night to save money, heat-damaging chocolate and other temperature-sensitive products during warm-weather months. For the Big Five, China's supply chain amounted to a gauntlet that their products had to run in order to simply be put in front of consumers.

During most of the 1990s, chocolate distribution reached fewer than 10,000 outlets throughout the country at the height of the summer months. During cool months, distribution would temporarily expand into non-air-conditioned stores—perhaps to five to seven times that number. Annual chocolate sales, therefore, fell into a boom-and-bust cycle that was exacerbated by the January–February timing of the Chinese New Year, China's largest gift-giving event of the year.[27] During the latter 1990s, Hershey's annual sales fell almost 40 percent within the two-month period prior to the New Year. As a result, chocolate companies invested significant time and effort each year filling the country's rickety non-air-conditioned supply-chain and retail stores. After the New Year, they then needed to support stock-clearance activities to sell out leftover stock in these stores before the onset of warm weather damaged the product. The lack of an extensive and reliable cool channel was one of the most significant limiting factors for the development of the chocolate market in China, and only added to chocolate company executives' preoccupation with the logistics aspect of their businesses, often to distraction.

* * * * *

American chocolate consumers pretty much know what they want when they enter the candy aisle of a food store, since

most of them typically make a beeline for their favorite chocolate bar. And at the cash register they demonstrate the same,
almost reflexive decision making when plucking their favorite
selection from the chocolate display rack. However, consumer
behavior in the chocolate aisles of China's supermarkets during the 1980s and 1990s was quite different. Consumers spent
significantly more time making their purchase decision.
There was a great deal of product handling: picking products
up; reading the back panel; comparing weights, prices, and
ingredients; and putting products back on the shelf. It was
obvious that Chinese consumers were still in the process of
acquiring basic knowledge about chocolate and chocolate
brands. They were a blank slate from the standpoints of chocolate brand awareness and taste preference, and for the Big
Five this was a rare and limited opportunity to establish their
brands as the preferred chocolate taste with China's first generation of chocolate consumers.

The emerging China market was a level playing field for all
of the Big Five when they arrived. Chinese consumers viewed
chocolate as an exotic foreign product, so each of the chocolate manufacturers enjoyed the same level of prestige and
credibility that China's inexperienced consumers associated
with foreign goods. Retail prices were relatively high and
manufacturing costs relatively low, so none found pricing and
cost to be barriers to entry. Importantly, each was flying blind
when it came to consumer and market information, and by
the seat of their pants when dealing with China's mercurial
economic and regulatory environment. And because chocolate was a low-interest product to the government, the Big
Five enjoyed a relatively high degree of freedom compared
to high-interest industries.[28] Finally, all enjoyed virtually no

credible local competition for over two decades. How their executives applied the experience, management skills, and leadership capabilities they brought to China would be decisive in how each approached the emerging consumer market and whether they ultimately succeeded.

Hershey was the most U.S. domestic oriented of the Big Five, and though it was a market leader in the relatively homogeneous American market, it did not have a proven track record in the more diverse and varied international marketplace—particularly in a complex emerging market like China. Mars, also an American company, had a much more established international presence and consequently a much broader base of experience to apply in China. Both Cadbury and Nestlé had been marketing chocolate around the world from just after the turn of the twentieth century, providing them greater depth and perspective from which to develop a successful approach to the China market. And Ferrero, a relative newcomer to retail chocolate, would prove to be the wild card of the group, with one of the most expensive and exotic chocolate products to offer.

As China's new consumer class emerged from the darkness into the stark fluorescent light of China's burgeoning retail stores, the best and the brightest minds of the global chocolate industry engaged each other in battle for their attention and affections. But it was not the trench warfare that these chocolate executives were accustomed to, sniping at each other from solid entrenchments in their well-established home markets. Rather, it was mobile warfare on a battlefield with a continually changing landscape that would test their skill, adaptability, and stamina, needed to win the hearts, minds, and wallets of the Chinese people.

Ferrero Rocher

Accidental Hero

China gave the world four great inventions: paper for writing, circa AD 100, and some nine hundred years later, movable type for printing, the magnetic compass, and gunpowder. Some would add pasta to that list, but the notion that explorer Marco Polo of Venice brought spaghetti back to Italy from China at the end of the thirteenth century is a popular misconception; there is overwhelming evidence that pasta had developed independently in both countries long before. But it was Marco Polo's father, Niccolò, and uncle, Maffeo, who undertook one of the earliest documented journeys of Europeans all the way to China's seat of power, Beijing, in 1266. Seven hundred years later, Italians would again be among the first to establish trade with China soon after it reopened its doors to the outside world in 1978. But this time, it would be the Ferrero family of Alba, Italy, instead of the Polos of Venice who would bear gifts of gold along the new "silk road" to China: Ferrero Rocher gold-foil-covered chocolate gift boxes.

Ferrero Rocher is a chocolate praline consisting of a single whole hazelnut floating in Nutella, a hazelnut-chocolate spread invented by family patriarch Pietro Ferrero, enclosed within a spherical wafer shell. The shell and its contents are dipped in chocolate and topped off with a sprinkle of hazelnut bits. Each individual treat is wrapped in a distinctive gold foil wrapper and sits in a chocolate-brown ruffled paper cup. The top of the plastic box in which they are sold is clear, allowing customers to see the lavishly wrapped delicacies within. If the race for the China chocolate market were a sprint and not a marathon, the clear winner would have been Ferrero. It was the first to establish its brand with China's emancipated consumers after the country reopened its doors to the outside world, and to this day Ferrero Rocher enjoys a special niche in the market there for high-end chocolate confections.

Some elderly Chinese will tell you that chocolate was not new to China in the early 1980s when Ferrero Rocher first arrived, and that they ate foreign brands of chocolate as schoolchildren in the 1930s. But this is a memory shared by only a fortunate few who came from prosperous families that lived either in or near colonial-era foreign enclaves. Similarly, some middle-aged Chinese recall crude homegrown forms of chocolate and chocolate-flavored sweets that were available in the 1970s. But since the economic privation of the 1950s through the 1970s and the Cultural Revolution effectively wiped clean the consumer-product slate during China's decades-long isolation from the outside world, by the early 1980s foreign chocolate brands were, for all intents and purposes, new products for nearly all Chinese people. And it was Ferrero Rocher that had the greatest early impact in establishing a first impression of chocolate on the nation's virgin chocolate consumers—an important and lasting impression. Ferrero Rocher was, simply, the global chocolate industry's first ambassador to China.

* * * * *

In postwar Italy, in the small, southern Piedmont village of Alba, Pietro Ferrero, a pastry shop owner, and his young son, Michele, began tinkering with confectionery concoctions. Nutella was the first product they developed that found a wide commercial market and is to Europeans what peanut butter is to Americans. Based on the commercial success of Nutella, Pietro Ferrero founded the Ferrero Company in 1946. Pietro died suddenly in 1949, and when young Michele had grown to adulthood, he donned the mantle of leadership of the company. The company rode on the singular success of Nutella until its blockbuster launch of TicTac mints in 1969, and it would be another thirteen years before it launched their now world-famous Ferrero Rocher chocolates. Today, Michele Ferrero still heads the family-owned Ferrero Company together with his wife, Maria Franca, and their sons, Pietro and Giovanni. Typical of many successful family-owned businesses, Ferrero's is tightly controlled, conservative, and secretive.

Pietro and son Michele shared a passion for originality

that is an integral part of the company's philosophy to this day. "Be unique! Never copy anyone else" is written into the company's mission statement. In this tradition, Michele Ferrero has personally led much of the company's product development over the decades and is credited with having invented Ferrero Rocher chocolates. From its humble beginnings, the Ferreros have grown their company into a food industry giant. Revenues in 2006 reached 5.6 billion Euros ($7 billion) and the company employs nearly 20,000 people worldwide.

Europeans know Ferrero best by its first, and still flagship, product, Nutella. Though created in 1946, it was first sold under the Nutella brand in 1964. Today it is one of the world's best-selling sweet spreads. Americans know Ferrero best by its famous TicTac brand mints. And Asians know Ferrero first and foremost as a chocolate company, primarily through Ferrero Rocher, the elaborate and elaborately packaged confection that first stirred so much affection for chocolate in China.

Though Ferrero Rocher is a far smaller business for Ferrero than Nutella, it is a chocolate gift-giving tradition in more than one hundred countries around the world. Importantly, unlike its confectionery rivals, Ferrero does not alter the Ferrero Rocher formula from market to market or country to country; the product is exactly the same whether you buy it in Boston, Berlin, or Beijing.

In chocolate terms, Ferrero Rocher is a relatively new product, introduced in 1982. By comparison, Hershey introduced the Kiss in 1907; Mars, as noted earlier, introduced the Milky Way bar in 1923; and Rowntree (now owned by Nestlé) introduced the KitKat in 1936.[1] Ferrero Rocher is one of the very few "new" chocolate products to establish and maintain a major presence in the global confectionery marketplace in recent decades. It is ironic, then, that Ferrero Rocher, a brand-new product, was one of the first foreign chocolates to enter China and to a large extent establish the image of what a chocolate product should be in the minds of the people.

Ferrero's Journey Along the Modern-Day Silk Road to China

Throughout the 1980s and early 1990s, cross-border trade flourished along the boundary between Hong Kong and China, and chocolate, along with consumer goods from around the world, arrived in contemporary China along the modern-day silk road that ran through the former British colony.

Until the Chinese Communist Revolution succeeded in 1949, Hong Kong was a sleepy colonial port city and home to an important British military base. The victory of Chinese Communist forces caused hundreds of thousands to flee from commercial cities such as Shanghai and Guangzhou to Hong Kong, including the cream of China's industrial and commercial class. In Hong Kong, these industrialists, together with the large influx of working-class people, found a strong laissez-faire policy toward business under the Hong Kong colonial government that served as the catalyst for Hong Kong's rapid industrialization and economic growth through the 1950s, 1960s, and 1970s. Hong Kong became not only a commercial and financial center but also a manufacturing powerhouse, turning out prodigious quantities of textiles and electronics, among other products. Thus, when China finally reopened its doors to the outside world in 1978, Hong Kong, being part of China (though still under lease to Great Britain at the time), and having well-established commercial contacts with the outside world and boasting one of the largest seaports in the world, was perfectly positioned to facilitate trade in and out of China. Hong Kong became a key gateway to China, through which businesspeople from around the world came to buy China's inexpensive merchandise. Furthermore, as Hong Kong manufacturers moved their factories into China, where labor was cheap, Hong Kong transformed itself from a manufacturing economy into more of a service economy. Throughout the 1980s and the early 1990s, most people traveling to China went through Hong Kong, banked with Hong Kong banks when purchasing goods made in China, and worked with Hong Kong trading companies in China; people in Hong Kong had the connections and spoke both Chinese and the international language of commerce.

With its newfound wealth, Hong Kong became a place known for its conspicuous consumption and excess. Some of Hong Kong's more extravagant restaurants would top off their dishes with a sprinkling of gold leaf, which was eagerly consumed by its status-conscious patrons with ivory chopsticks. In such an environment, a luxury chocolate such as Ferrero Rocher was a natural. Although most of its citizens could not afford the $30,000 jewel-encrusted gold Swiss Rolex watches or the Mercedes-Benz cars that filled shop windows along Hong Kong's narrow streets, nearly all could afford an Italian gold-colored Ferrero Rocher chocolate gift box. For those aspiring to a higher station in life, Ferrero Rocher was a symbol of the good life.

Ferrero introduced Ferrero Rocher in Hong Kong almost immediately after its launch in 1982. Made in Italy, it was sold through one of Hong Kong's leading imported food distributors, J.D. Hutchison, which was assigned as Ferrero Rocher's exclusive distributor owing to its extensive distribution network throughout Hong Kong. As the old consumer marketing saying goes, "Stack it high and watch it fly," and fly it did. During the Chinese New Year's festival, Ferrero Rocher's presence in Hong Kong's food stores was ubiquitous. Watson's, a leading retail chain store, would literally stack boxes of Ferrero Rocher floor to ceiling in spectacular displays that occupied a large share of its precious retail space. With its gold color symbolizing wealth and good fortune in the Chinese culture, and its elaborate packaging, in a few short years Ferrero Rocher became a mainstay of Hong Kong's gifting tradition. With Hong Kong serving as the port of entry on the modern-day silk road for consumer products arriving in China, it was only a matter of time until the cachet of Ferrero Rocher crossed the border and captured the fancy of China's emerging and impressionable consumer class.

China's Emancipated Consumers

Prior to 1978, people in China were provided with state-approved idols and role models, whose sole purpose was to exalt the virtues of the Communist Revolution. Aside from well-known icons such as Chairman Mao Zedong, the Chinese Communist Party made idols of common people as well. Lei Feng was not a politician or glamorous movie star, nor a musician or performer of any kind. He was a simple soldier. Orphaned, then raised by the Communist Party faithful, he became a soldier and died in a banal work accident in 1962. The Chinese Communist Party picked up the story, and through a series of propaganda campaigns that began in 1963 with "Learn from Comrade Lei Feng," his image and tales of his selfless exploits in service to the people of China were relentlessly broadcast to China's population through the state-controlled media. As a consequence, during the 1960s and 1970s he became the hero of millions of Chinese people. Chinese people coming of age when the door to China cracked open at the end of the 1970s, however, were virtual sponges for the exotic sights, sounds, and tastes of what was, until then, very much the outside world, and movie stars and other pop icons quickly supplanted China's state-sponsored heroes.

Their passion for all things foreign, especially Western culture, became clear to me when I first started working for Hershey in China in 1998 and met the marketing manager, a Chinese man who introduced himself to me as David Wham. There are thousands of Chinese surnames in use in China; most of them are monosyllabic. Still, I had never heard the family name Wham in China, and it struck me as odd. I soon learned that David's family name was actually Wan, but after China hosted its first Western pop concert tour in 1985, by the British band Wham! featuring singer George Michael, David was so impressed by the promotional images he saw from the event that he adopted the band's name. For people of David's generation, posthumous images of Lei Feng striking an action hero pose and clad in his revolutionary uniform, red star on his hat, rifle slung across his shoulder, simply could not compete with George Michael in his black leather jacket, cross-shaped earring, sunglasses, and three days' growth of beard.

Michael was the antithesis of Lei, a veritable rainbow of color in an otherwise drab society. What was true for entertainment icons was also true for consumer products like Ferrero Rocher, and anything coming across the border from Hong Kong was immediately met with fascination born of curiosity for the new.

Among the first outsiders to come to China with the reopening of the country were well-heeled Hong Kong businessmen, many of whom established small manufacturing industries in China's special economic zones such as Shenzhen and nearby Zhuhai. As the first point of contact with the outside world for many Mainland Chinese people, they became an important symbol of success to be admired, envied, and even emulated in China. And many of them brought gifts to China, including Ferrero Rocher, to develop both personal and business relationships. Further, the vast majority of Hong Kong residents are descendents of Cantonese Chinese (Guangdong Province), speak the Cantonese Chinese dialect as their mother tongue, and have extended families who live in China. As travel restrictions eased in the early 1980s, Hong Kong people would cross the border en mass to attend family gatherings, particularly during the Chinese New Year festival. Nearly all of them were bearing gifts for their relatives, and the most popular food gifts to be brought across the border in this way were the so-called Hong Kong Big Four: Kjeldsens Butter Cookies (blue tin); Sugus chewy candies (red tin); Almond Roca almond-toffee sweets (pink tin); and the most prized, Ferrero Rocher chocolates (gold box). These Hong Kong gift traditions and customs were eagerly adopted, particularly by the 80 million Chinese living in Guangdong, and this was the genesis of Ferrero Rocher's link with China and its gift-giving traditions.

Establishing a Route-to-Market in China

By the mid-1980s, the demand for Ferrero Rocher and other consumer products was there, but China's impenetrable, tangled mess of bureaucratic regulations and arbitrarily applied import duties kept most goods, including Ferrero Rocher, from being imported for sale. Throughout the 1980s, China had an outright ban on the issuance of importing, trading, and wholesaling licenses to foreign companies. The situation was even too much for Hong Kong's great import and export trading houses, such as Jardine Matheson and Company and Swire Pacific (fictionalized as Straun and Company and Rothwell-Gornt, respectively, in James Clavell's 1981 novel *Nobel House*), J.D. Hutchison, and a host of lesser trading companies, to overcome.

Ironically, some of these aforementioned trading companies peddled opium to China in the 1800s, and it was China's experience with these companies, and the pernicious effects of opium on Chinese society, that contributed to China's wariness of open trade borders. The 1700s and 1800s were dark days for China and its relationships with the outside world. Opium addiction was widespread there and the British East India Company, the era's most powerful trading company, commanded a virtual monopoly on the opium trade into China, albeit indirectly. Up to the mid-1800s, it was banned in China and the British East India Company refrained from violating the ban, perhaps because it operated under British Royal Charter and acted in a governmental capacity for the British government in the region. It therefore purchased opium in India, sold it in the markets of Calcutta, no questions asked, and it was then up to trading companies such as Jardine Matheson and Company to find a way to smuggle it into China. It is entirely understandable, then, that China would not simply throw open its doors to foreign trading companies once again, some of which actually made their early fortunes in the opium trade.

In the 1980s, though J.D. Hutchison (not one of the former opium smugglers) did a good job of distributing Ferrero Rocher in Hong Kong, it could do little in the way of building a distribution network for the product across the border in China. The limitations placed on Ferrero's Hong Kong distributor in China are important, since a product's commercial destiny is inexorably tied to the capabilities and performance of its distributor. However, in Hong Kong's freewheeling capitalist economy, no demand would go unmet, and it would be up to entrepreneurial Hong Kong freelance traders with both strong constitutions and strong relationships on the China side of the border to find a more effective and efficient way into China for Ferrero Rocher.

In the mid-1980s, these traders and their counterparts on the China side of the border operated a so-called gray-market channel into China through ports in close proximity to Hong Kong, such as Shenzhen and Zhuhai. Like the British East India Company in Calcutta over 150 years earlier, Hong Kong distributors would sell products to these freelancers in Hong Kong, no questions asked. How the freelancers got the goods through customs, whether import duties were paid, and how the freelancers got paid by their buyers were anybody's guess. These business practices were not taught in business schools, not published in the business section of Hong Kong's *South China Morning Post* daily newspaper, nor was the topic openly discussed. Business grew steadily, so no one along the gray-market supply chain was complaining.

In 1990, J.D. Hutchison was purchased by Inchcape, another venerable European-Asian trading house whose roots stretch back to the nineteenth century. With the acquisition, the firm became Inchcape JDH. During the next three years, Ferrero Rocher's sales in China grew steadily, but the product continued to enter China through the gray-market channel owing to the licensing ban to foreign companies. In 1993, Inchcape JDH made an important move that would be the first step in improving Ferrero Rocher's route-to-market: it established a representative office in China. Though still not permitted to do import, trade, or wholesale, it employed an in-house team of liaison representatives whose activities were limited to what was termed "distribution pull-through marketing," which consisted chiefly of building relationships with local distributors and retailers and encouraging sales of the products they distributed. While Inchcape JDH was still unable to act as a fully operational distributor on behalf of Ferrero, this was an important milestone for the development of the Ferrero Rocher business in China because the product was now able to be actively marketed and promoted there.

In 1995, Ferrero Rocher's destiny in the China market took another favorable turn when Inchcape JDH became one of the first foreign trading companies to acquire a trading and wholesaling license. This allowed Ferrero to take an even greater degree of control over its business by providing better management and coordination of distribution and marketing activities for its brand. Still, no foreign trading company would be issued an import license during the 1990s, so the services of a Chinese importing agent would continue to be required. Ferrero would sell Ferrero Rocher to Inchcape JDH in Hong Kong, which would in turn sell it to a licensed Chinese import agent. Inchcape JDH's China subsidiary would then buy the goods back from the import agent and resell them to wholesalers and city distributors, many of which were mom-and-pop operations whose territory covered part or all of a particular city. Like the silk road of old, the modern route-to-market road was a long and convoluted path with products passing through many hands. However, this jerry-rigged system did the job. In spite of this complexity, Inchcape JDH managed to forge a structured distribution system in China that helped boost overall distribution of Ferrero Rocher and greatly accelerated its brand awareness across the country.

Throughout the late 1980s and first half of the 1990s, nearly all of Ferrero Rocher's retail sales in China occurred through a very limited number, perhaps only a few hundred, of high-end state-owned department stores and supermarkets. These were the only suitable retail outlets that existed for Ferrero Rocher at the time. However, by the mid-1990s, China's retail sector began to develop rapidly, and during the second half of the decade, retailers such as the French hypermarket (superstore) retail giant Carrefour, and to a lesser extent Wal-Mart, along with an agglomeration of high-quality local hypermarkets and supermarkets, began to appear on the scene in China's main first-tier cities. Each new store opening essentially expanded the number of accessible consumers, and this, in turn, grew the chocolate market in China. In order to better manage this emerging opportunity in China's evolving retail sector, Ferrero established a representative office in China but maintained a small footprint with only twenty to thirty in-country liaison representatives. Located in first-tier cities such as Beijing, Shanghai, and Guangzhou, their job was to watch over Inchcape JDH's distribution execution and to direct marketing and promotion activities in these retail stores.

Because Ferrero Rocher was purchased as a gift, marketing activities and promotions were almost exclusively focused on the traditional gift-giving festivals. Given the timing of these festivals, and the weather, selling Ferrero Rocher fell into a seasonal cycle. With only a limited number of air-conditioned retail stores and no significant summer-season gift-giving festivals, sales would drop to near zero during the summer months. The selling cycle would begin a month or so before the Mid-Autumn Festival, a 3,000-year-old traditional harvest celebration that is often referred to as the Mooncake Festival, for the Chinese mooncakes[2] people would consume during the holiday. Based on the lunar calendar, the festival occurs when the moon is full and brightest in the sky during the month of September, so the exact date fluctuates from year to year between the middle and the end of September. Accordingly, Ferrero would start filling the distribution pipeline in mid- to late August. Because the weather is still quite warm throughout most of China at this time, distribution focused mainly on air-conditioned stores where the product would not melt.

After the Mid-Autumn Festival, the level of Ferrero Rocher's distribution in retail stores would gradually increase throughout the fall months with the onset of cooler weather.

A second major distribution push would begin in December for the Chinese New Year Festival, also known as Spring Festival. Another lunar calendar holiday, it occurs between mid-January and mid-February and is the main gift-giving event of the year.

Following the fifteen-day Chinese New Year's festival, distribution and marketing efforts would immediately switch from maximizing distribution to inventory clearance, not unlike what happens with Halloween candy in the United States in early November each year. For chocolate, the imperative was to get whatever product remained in non-air-conditioned outlets sold before the arrival of hot weather in May. Though distributors were largely responsible for dealing with any peak-season leftovers, the cost of product returns was shared by Ferrero as a cost of doing business in China's hyperseasonal chocolate gift market. The market was then virtually dead during the summer months, except for sales in some key air-conditioned outlets, until the cycle began again in August in anticipation of the next Mid-Autumn Festival.

Ferrero drove both peak-season sales and stock clearance mainly through funding special retail displays and in-store promoters[3] in key stores, and Inchcape JDH would carry out activities such as display-building competitions with its sales and merchandising people to get displays built and have them well maintained during the season. Also, with the low cost of in-store merchandising labor, it was cost-effective to pay for Inchcape JDH's merchandisers to fan out to retail stores and put seasonal sleeves over Ferrero Rocher gift boxes in order to "seasonalize" them for the Mid-Autumn and New Year's festivals. These sleeves were typically made of paper and had a holiday imprint, such as a stylized moon image and a "Happy

Moon Festival" message for the Mid-Autumn Festival. When the holiday was over, merchandisers would go through stores and pull the sleeves off, only to place new, holiday-appropriate sleeves on them as a new holiday approached.

In one instance, China's procedure-heavy regulatory environment actually gave Ferrero and other foreign food importers a competitive advantage, albeit inadvertently. Throughout the 1980s and 1990s, a holographic circular sticker needed to be fixed to all imported food products to identify them to regulators, retailers, and consumers as an import. A Chinese-language product-information label also needed to be adhered to the product if it didn't already have a multilanguage label. One of the jobs of the licensed importer was to open shipping cases and place the import sticker and product-information label on every item. It was worth the effort because China's emerging consumers held imported products in high regard, and foreign companies whose products bore the import sticker could charge a substantial premium. The sticker and label, though required by law, thus became important marketing tools.

Ferrero Rocher also took hold in China because Ferrero was vigilant about product quality and took extensive measures to maintain condition and freshness. No product over six months old was delivered to retail stores, and product that was three months before expiration date was pulled from shelves. Among their other duties, Ferrero's liaison representatives in China would go to retail stores, survey expiration dates, and pick up aging product. With the cost of returns and unsold product shared by Ferrero and its distribution partners, all links in the supply chain had an incentive to keep the freshest possible product in front of consumers by, for example, taking more care to ensure proper rotation of stock in warehouses throughout the supply chain.

As Ferrero became more established in China, it sought other ways to make its operations there more economical. For instance, most of the Ferrero Rocher SKUs[4] sold in China were the sixteen- and twenty-four-piece gift boxes. The two key components of the box—the clear plastic box top and the brown opaque bottom—could be produced less expensively in China than in Europe. Consequently, as China became a major worldwide exporter of packaging materials, it made no sense for Ferrero to buy packaging made in China, ship it to Italy to be packed by expensive European labor only to be shipped back to Hong Kong, China, and other Asian Pacific markets for sale. Therefore, starting in the 1990s, Ferrero began shipping some of its Ferrero Rocher product in bulk for final packing in Hong Kong.

As of the writing of this book, Ferrero's route-to-market in China continues to rely on a trading and distribution partner, with **SIMS** Trading taking over this role from Inchcape in 2001. This third-party business model makes sense for Ferrero, given the size of its business and the extreme seasonal fluctuation of the chocolate gift business itself in China; it avoids maintaining a large infrastructure that will be idle during parts of the year.

Ferrero's Struggle with Local Copycats

Until it reopened its doors in 1978, the concept of intellectual property rights in China was virtually nonexistent, and the reason for its conspicuous absence went well beyond the fact that private property was virtually eliminated after communism took hold in 1949. The concept of intellectual property and its ownership rights has deep roots in European history and tradition. Patents can be traced back to the Greeks, circa 500 BC, with the first modern patent originating in Venice, Italy, in the 1400s. Trademarks first appeared in Europe in the 1200s and copyrights after the arrival of the printing press in Europe in the 1600s. In the modern-day Western world these have become well-established legal traditions that are handed down to American schoolchildren when they are taught about Thomas Edison and Alexander Bell and their famous inventions and patents. Because China's society developed independently from that of Europe's, and did not follow this same path of intellectual property rights development, the concept of intellectual property rights is still quite new there. As a result, copying of foreign products in China has been a problem of epidemic proportions, and it is still very much an evolving feature of this market. And for the privilege of being the first of the Big Five chocolate companies in China, Ferrero would also be a pioneer in facing this cultural and historical gap head-on.

It is ironic that Ferrero's motto is "Be unique! Never copy anyone else" since, perhaps more than any other foreign chocolate company in China, it has been plagued by one of the most long-lived and notorious cases of local copycatting. In 1982, Ferrero filed its import registration under both the foreign language name, Ferrero Rocher, and a Chinese name, Jinsha.[5] But when it applied for trademark registration in 1986, it only registered its foreign language name with the Chinese Trademark Office. This procedural oversight set in motion a chain of events that nearly caused Ferrero to lose its unique product to a local copycat.

If imitation is the greatest form of flattery, then Zhangjia-gang Dairy Factory One, seeing the success that Ferrero Rocher was having with China's consumers, decidedly flattered Michele Ferrero by producing its own copy of it. As the saying goes, "Use it or lose it," and Zhangjiagang Dairy applied for and received trademark approval for the Chinese name Jinsha in 1990 for its Ferrero Rocher knockoff. When the company attempted to register the combination of the Jin-sha name with its Ferrero Rocher look-alike brand label, Ferrero objected, and that objection was upheld by the China Trademark Office. In spite of this, Zhangjiagang Dairy continued to use the Jinsha name along with the label.

Zhangjiagang Dairy was not the only company to copy Ferrero Rocher in China, though its Jinsha brand was by far the highest-quality and most successful copy on the market. Several low-grade versions of the product also appeared over the years. One memorable one was a poorly made Ferrero Rocher copy whose unappetizing foreign language name was "Fretate Relish." The intent was to impress less discerning Chinese chocolate consumers by using any foreign language words that conveniently consisted of a seven-letter word that began with *F* followed by a six-letter word that began with *R*. Ferrero took action against low-grade copycats such as these through the State Administration on Industry and Commerce, Trademark Office, one of the primary intellectual property (IP) enforcement agencies in China that will act on behalf of brand owners to enforce IP rights and that had the authority to shut down copycat operations. However, most of these low-grade copycat companies are fly-by-night operations that will have their doors locked by authorities one day only to pop up under a different company name and literally just down the street a few days later. In this respect, dealing with copycat companies in China was like the Whac-a-Mole gopher bash game: a copycat would pop up out of a hole, and as soon as you whacked him down, another one would pop up and after you whacked him down, another would pop up, and so on.

However, Zhangjiagang Dairy was a special case because it was a legitimate company with established operations in other lines of business, such as milk and milk by-products. Whereas most local copycats were content to make a quick buck while keeping a low profile, focusing on less conspicuous retail outlets in major cities and driving their distribution into third- and fourth-tier cities, Zhangjiagang Dairy boldly targeted the same first-tier cities and high-end retail stores as Ferrero, even selling in China's international airport duty-free shops. Jinsha eventually developed a wide consumer following, with sales that compared with those of Ferrero Rocher. Side by side on the retail shelf, at first glance it was difficult to tell Ferrero's Ferrero Rocher apart from Zhangjiagang Dairy's Jinsha. Both companies could demonstrate that they operated legitimate businesses, and this meant that each could sue the other under China's Unfair Competition Law. This law protects a company's IP rights if the product is well known and makes it unlawful for another company to sell a similar product that would cause confusion in the market. But who was the "owner" and who was the "infringer"? If Ferrero pursued the case, it would be a foreign company's attempting to shut down a hometown favorite, in which case Ferrero would face a real possibility of being ordered to refrain from selling Ferrero Rocher in China because it interfered with Jinsha!

During the decade-long battle between Ferrero and Zhangjiagang Dairy, Ferrero struggled with direct side-by-side competition with its local rival, with Jinsha selling at a substantially lower price. While the legal process played itself out, Ferrero had to take action with consumers, with the real battleground being in retail stores, not the courthouse.

Ferrero encouraged its in-store merchandisers and retailers to separate the two products on the retail shelf as much as possible to minimize consumers' making side-by-side comparisons. Also, Ferrero took great pains to talk to retail buyers to educate them about the pitfalls of selling "fake" product in their stores. This argument was strengthened after 2000, with the emergence of a number of high-profile consumer-poisoning cases, one tragically involving fake locally made baby formula that had too little nutritional value, which led to the malnourishment of hundreds of babies and to the deaths of over fifty babies in 2004.[6] Retailers knew that Zhangjiagang Dairy's Jinsha was not a fake, but a legal brand and a product in its own right. Ferrero's most compelling argument to retailers was that they should not sell Zhangjiagang Dairy's Jinsha since, owing to Ferrero's higher price, retailers made more money, gift box for gift box, with Ferrero Rocher. While this may have been true, it was in fact the least persuasive argument, since most retailers decided to continue to sell both Ferrero Rocher and Zhangjiagang Dairy's Jinsha—and for a very good reason: consumers demanded both.

Over the first two decades of China's transformational era, consumers had become accustomed to copycat products of all kinds, not just food. Having come of age as consumers throughout the topsy-turvy experimental phase of China's transformational era, and through the rapidly accelerating consumerism throughout the 1990s in particular, many Chinese consumers have taken the copycat phenomenon in stride. Not knowing any different, they accepted it as just a natural feature of the free market; it became a part of daily life.

There is no question that Jinsha had an impact on Ferrero Rocher sales in China; however, to what degree this is so is debatable and nearly impossible to quantify. This is because, although Ferrero Rocher and its Jinsha rival may have looked alike, their vastly different price meant that they competed for different segments of the market. In other words, a large percentage of Jinsha buyers would not step up and pay the high price of Ferrero Rocher if Jinsha were unavailable in the store.

Ferrero was, of course, not alone in its battle with China's copycats. Nestlé China, for example, has hundreds of products, ranging from infant formula to coffee, and maintains a well-staffed legal department at its Greater China Region Headquarters in Beijing that, among other legal work such as product registration and licensing, is continually pursuing and challenging copiers of its products. The cost of defending IP in China is substantial, but the cost of doing nothing, in terms of both lost sales and long-term degradation of its brands, would certainly be much higher.

In 2005, Ferrero took the risk and pursued its case against Zhangjiagang Dairy on the basis of its similarity to Ferrero Rocher causing consumer confusion. Though it was eventually ruled that Ferrero Rocher was, in fact, copied by Zhangjiagang Dairy without its authorization, as of the writing of this book both can still be found side by side in retail stores. Ultimately, both Ferrero and Jinsha found a home with Chinese consumers.

Did Ferrero Succeed in China?

Ferrero is not the chocolate leader in China. However, in spite of its challenges in the IP arena, Ferrero's entry into China can be viewed as nothing short of successful. Having made the earliest significant impact on consumers' perceptions in China's fledgling chocolate market with its Ferrero Rocher gift boxes, it succeeded in establishing a first impression of chocolate as a luxurious and exotic foreign confection that not only reflected the buyer's (giver's) good taste but also became a symbol of permissive indulgence for people emerging from lifestyles of extreme thrift. This alone is a remarkable accomplishment. Furthermore, having found its way through China's transformational era, Ferrero Rocher has become a fixture in the confectionery market today, having stood the test of time.

Ferrero's success in China can largely be attributed to its aggressive introduction of Ferrero Rocher into the Chinese festival gift-giving culture. Self-consumption would become more prevalent beginning in the late 1990s, and in this respect Ferrero Rocher did not suffer the early growing pains of its competitors, who struggled to push their products into a mass market of consumers whose chocolate self-consumption habits were in their infancy. Ferrero faced this same challenge with its Nutella brand, for example, which never took off in China because it is primarily a spread for bread, and the simple fact is that few Chinese eat bread and even fewer eat bread with a spread. Like chocolate for self-consumption, Nutella simply didn't fit with Chinese consumption habits.

Ferrero also set the bar high in terms of consumer expectations by imprinting a high-quality (and high-price) consumer expectation, and establishing and promoting a "chocolate mystique" among consumers. One of the ways it accomplished this was through airing its "Ambassador" television ad. It featured a butler presenting an ambassador (both Europeans standing in a lavish setting) with a silver platter piled high with Ferrero Rocher chocolates for his approval for serving at the evening's high-society gala. The ambassador approves with a flamboyant display of compliments for Ferrero Rocher, as do the guests as they arrive at the gala. This kind of image building with Chinese consumers not only served Ferrero well but its multinational competitors as well and allowed the entire China chocolate market, both the gift-giving and self-consumption segments, to develop under a premium image. Local competition, which could not meet these quality expectations, was largely kept at bay for over twenty years.

Ferrero's focus on the premium and gift-giving segments hit the chocolate "sweet spot" in the China market, which consisted of selected distribution in high-end retail outlets where chocolate was being purchased, seasonal events when chocolate was being purchased, and the pockets and gift expense accounts of those who were capable of paying up to two days' wages (for an average big-city office worker) for a luxury item.

At the same time, despite another popular slogan at the Ferrero company, "Making quality confectionery a part of every day life," it has thus far failed to make Ferrero Rocher a part of daily life in China. Although Ferrero has tried to enter the self-consumption segment of the market with Ferrero Rocher, it has had very limited success. Ferrero sells paper-tray and shrink-wrapped three- and five-packs of Ferrero Rocher, targeted at this market and placed at impulse-purchase locations (e.g., cash registers) in retail stores. However, China's value-conscious consumers are willing to pay high prices for Ferrero Rocher as a gift for others, but not as a treat for themselves.[7] Further, competition in the self-consumption segment is intense, and without its distinctive packaging, Ferrero Rocher had little competitive advantage over players such as Cadbury, Hershey, Nestlé, and Mars. Most important, Ferrero was too well established as a gift in consumers' minds to credibly make the leap into self-consumption.

The Ferrero family had a long-term vision for the China market, and they were consistent and disciplined in their approach to the evolving China opportunity. As a family-owned business it was not at the mercy of stockholders demanding short-term returns. The latter often forces the hand of publicly listed companies into short-term decision making as a result of factors that have nothing whatsoever to do with building a business in China, or business performance in general. If, for example, profitability was down in China owing to higher than expected market returns in a particular year, the family could decide to accept it for what it was, learn from it, and move on. In some public companies, however, it is a fact of life that financial planning and budgetary rules put in place to govern the business may dictate automatic corrective measures such as a price increase or a marketing budget cut in order to deliver a financial number that had been committed to the faceless ownership of the stock market, regardless of its long-term impact on the business.

Furthermore, public companies are led by professional managers (as opposed to family members), and since international job assignments to a market like China tend to be short stopovers on their career path, past lessons are lost and perceptions change with each successive manager. On its own, a single corrective measure or change of leadership is unlikely to bring a business to its knees, but cumulatively, over time, these can steer a business significantly off course. Free from this constraint, the Ferrero family consistently implemented both their strategy and their execution for the business in China.

Consistency of strategy is, of course, easier when you know what works to begin with, and much tougher when you are groping in the dark for the right formula for success, as other chocolate companies did during the first two decades of China's transformational era. When Ferrero Rocher achieved overnight success in Hong Kong, and subsequently in China's border towns, it was obvious that its unique marketing mix of product, price, packaging, promotion, and brand image worked— and worked exceptionally well in a Chinese context. The Ferreros knew they had a hit on their hands, and they wisely chose to stay the course with this approach. Its overall strategy for China was straightforward: roll out the success achieved in Hong Kong into China; no more, no less.

Initially, sales volume was not as high a priority as setting distribution targets and driving its business partners, Inchcape JDH and later SIMS Trading, to achieve them. Distribution was Ferrero Rocher's main business development lever. It held on to its premium pricing strategy, even with Jinsha selling for as much as 50 percent less. Ferrero surmised that any price reduction would diminish the brand image it was working so hard to establish. While some savings could be had by repacking in Hong Kong, the locally sourced packaging materials had to continue to meet Ferrero's high standards, and there would be no compromise on packaging, either.

The company also kept a tight grip on its marketing funds and always sought more economical methods of promotion and advertising. It was one of the few companies to aggres-sively exploit print advertising early on, which is arguably a more effective medium for a seasonal gift item than for an everyday impulse-purchase item. And when Ferrero did tele-vision advertising, it not only used the same television com-mercial that was used worldwide with a Chinese voice-over, but it used the same ad year after year.

Ferrero wasn't willing to experiment with its successful product or marketing mix for China, nor was it prepared to reinvent its management style. Ferrero kept its Asia opera-tions both lean and on a tight leash. Its Asia headquarters in Hong Kong was overseen by senior directors who flew in from Italy once a quarter. Its in-market employees focused on en-suring distribution execution, product freshness, and quality, and on building consumer brand awareness for Ferrero Rocher. And its distributors like SIMS Trading were exe-cuters, not decision makers. This rigid orthodoxy provided a highly stable management structure that ensured consistent effort in distribution, in-store merchandising and promotion, and consumer communication—all critical to successfully building a consumer-product brand.

Ferrero likely could have achieved more with Ferrero Rocher in China. Sales of Ferrero Rocher are greatly concen-trated in southern China—over half of its total national sales. This implies that there are unrealized opportunities in the rest of the country. Conversely, Ferrero's success is attributable in part to its avoidance of overreaching.

Overreach has been a major trap for many multinational companies operating in China, typically in the form of push-ing a product into a city or region without adequate market-ing support or distribution management. Directives from the head office, underperforming business operations, margin erosion, and even overzealous glory seeking all contribute to the pressure to push beyond sustainable limits. Unfortunately, the retail and distribution trade in China has become unforgiving in this regard. In the 1980s and early 1990s, foreign brands carried a great deal of prestige and were coveted commodities by Chinese distributors and retailers. But once a product falls from grace by acquiring a reputation for poor performance, the manufacturer can count on a long, slow climb back to credibility—if rehabilitation is possible at all.

The dusty roads of China are littered with the bones of companies that came to China for a quick sales hit, overestimated the achievable opportunity in China, and overextended their businesses; Ferrero was not one of them. It knew its product was exceptionally expensive for the market, and consequently did not expect to sell Ferrero Rocher to a billion people there. It also understood the nature of the opportunity before it, it remained disciplined, and it focused like a laser on the market sweet spot. Ferrero's twenty-five-year adventure has fulfilled the aspirations of Michele Ferrero and his family—and that, in the end, is how the company measures its success.

* * * * *

As the hand of communism and central planning relaxed its grip on economic activity in China, and the critical-mass phase of China's transformation began to gear up in the 1990s, the nation's chocolate landscape would change dramatically within just a few years. Between 1993 and 1996, Mars and Cadbury would build chocolate factories in Beijing, and Nestlé would build another in Tianjin (a northern port city near

Beijing). Cadbury, Nestlé, and Mars focused on products that would be consumed by the purchaser (rather than be given as a gift) year-round, and the sales of their products were far less seasonal than Ferrero Rocher's. With a year-round business that provided a steadier and thus higher percentage of production-capacity utilization, along with not incurring import duties, producing chocolate for self-consumption in China, where labor and material costs are lower, would be more efficient and substantially reduce costs. They, therefore, saw in-market manufacturing as an essential element in their China business models, unlike Ferrero. Only Hershey, the other Big Five chocolate company to build a China business model based on imported products in the 1990s, would push back from in-country manufacturing and follow the distribution and marketing–driven business model as Ferrero did.

At the same time, as David Wham's generation of consumers began to emerge in China's big cities, they developed a taste for the occasional pizza, McDonald's hamburger, and Kentucky Fried Chicken. With pocket money to spend on small luxury items, this new generation was the pioneer consumer class for the development of China's self-consumption chocolate market. The good news for Ferrero was that the entire chocolate market grew. The purchase of chocolate for self-consumption didn't come at the expense of the gift market.

With the advent of in-country chocolate manufacturing and growing year-round demand for chocolate, by the mid-1990s the Hong Kong silk road through southern China was no longer the center of chocolate commerce. However, to this day, Ferrero Rocher continues to be imported to China along this route, though the once thriving gray market has for the most part become black and white.

Having invested the effort and resources that it did over a decade of remaining vigilant in defending its intellectual property in China, it is not surprising that Ferrero would be more than a little gun-shy when considering exposing its proprietary Ferrero Rocher formula and production processes to being copied in China. Further, for a hyperseasonal product like Ferrero Rocher, the same efficiencies that apply to using third-party distributors apply to manufacturing—it would be highly inefficient for Ferrero to have a manufacturing plant in China sitting virtually idle for half the year. For these reasons, it is unlikely that we will see a Ferrero Rocher factory in China in the foreseeable future.

* * * * *

As a brand-new chocolate product, not created with Chinese consumers in mind, Ferrero Rocher happened to be perfectly suited to Chinese tastes and gifting traditions. Initially hand carried into China from Hong Kong by people visiting their families across the border, it was eagerly adopted by the country's virgin chocolate consumers and essentially pulled into the China market, an opportunity that the Ferrero family was successful in capitalizing upon. It was therefore serendipitous that Ferrero Rocher achieved the rapid success that it did, coming into being precisely at the time when China's chocolate consumers were most ready to receive this gift all the way from Alba, Italy. Ferrero Rocher was the accidental hero of China's fledgling chocolate market. However, things would not be so easy for its main competitors—Cadbury, Hershey, Nestlé, and Mars—when they took up the battle for China's chocolate consumers.

CHAPTER 3

Cadbury

One Billion Consumers

I n the tradition of the overreaching ambitions that nineteenth-century British colonial haberdashers held for the China market, British chocolate maker Cadbury entered the market with an intriguing, if idealistic, strategy: to sell a Cadbury Dairy Milk Chocolate bar to each of the country's 1 billion people.[1] While this was, of course, a fanciful proposition, it reflected Cadbury's belief that it was one of the best positioned of the Big Five chocolate companies to become market leader in China when the country opened its doors to the outside world in the late 1970s.

Cadbury was the first of the companies to tie its fortunes to the cocoa bean, albeit with chocolate and cocoa beverages during the first half of the nineteenth century. It was also one of the world's first global chocolate companies, expanding its operations outside of Great Britain during the 1920s and 1930s.[2] By 1939, it operated factories on four continents: Europe, North America (in Canada), Australia, and Africa (in South Africa). The storied adage "The sun never sets on the British Empire" was also true of Cadbury. Wherever the British Empire went, so too did Cadbury chocolate, and British colonies in cities such as Hong Kong and Shanghai gave Cadbury access to the Chinese people and made it the dominant chocolate brand in China during the colonial era. With its global business savvy and longtime market leadership in India, a former British colony that, like China, was a developing country with a huge population, Cadbury appeared perfectly positioned to become the number-one chocolate brand in China during the 1980s and 1990s.

A Brief History of Cadbury Chocolate

In 1824, a young Englishman named John Cadbury opened a grocery store in Birmingham, and by 1831 he was making and selling chocolate and cocoa beverages. His brother, Benjamin, joined the family business in 1847, and the company became known as Cadbury Brothers. Cadbury Brothers was one of the early pioneers in cocoa's making its gradual transition from a beverage, as it had been consumed for thousands of years, to solid chocolate. In 1849, the Cadbury brothers made the company's first eating chocolate, though its taste and texture were nothing like the smooth and creamy chocolate we know and love today. The product was not a commercial success.

In the early 1850s, John Cadbury's sons, Richard and George, joined the family business, and in 1854 they received a Royal Warrant of Appointment, which allowed them to prominently display the Royal Coat of Arms on their product's packaging, certifying that the company was a supplier of cocoa products to the British royal family. The Cadbury sons eventually took over the business in 1861, and five years later the company's solid milk chocolate development took an important step forward with George's purchase of a cocoa press from Holland. The new press allowed for the separation of cocoa butter from the cocoa mass, which enabled experimentation with various combinations of ingredients and formulas. But it would take more than thirty years before the Cadbury brothers developed their first viable formula for milk chocolate, in 1897, and another eight years until the Cadburys hit on their now famous Cadbury Dairy Milk Chocolate formula, which incorporates "a glass and a half of milk in every half pound of milk chocolate," the company's slogan for its milk chocolate bars to this day.

Cadbury's Dairy Milk Chocolate became the company's number-one product line by 1913 and remains its flagship brand. By today's standards Cadbury's new-product development progressed slowly. Though it launched its Dairy Milk Chocolate brand in 1905, its next product, Milk Tray assorted boxed chocolates, wasn't launched until 1915, and Cadbury Crème Eggs, until 1923. Two variations of its famous Cadbury Dairy Milk Chocolate followed: Cadbury Fruit and Nut bar, launched in 1928, with its Cadbury Whole Nut bar coming along in 1933. Cadbury Roses twist-wrapped boxed chocolates were launched in 1938.

Cadbury remained a family-run business until it went

public in 1962, when the company became known as Cadbury Limited. Flush with new capital, Cadbury further expanded its product offerings to include toffees by acquiring in 1964 the Éclairs brand from British confectioner James Pascall. Éclairs are bite-size toffee treats with a chocolate center and have become one of Cadbury's most successful confectionery products.

In 1969, Cadbury Limited merged with the beverage powerhouse Schweppes, becoming the global confectionery and beverages company Cadbury Schweppes, with well-known beverage brands such as Schweppes Club Soda, Snapple, and Dr. Pepper. Cadbury Schweppes tried, but failed, to make its sizable confectionery business a success in the United States, in large part because it could not compete with American companies Hershey and Mars on their own turf. Unable to beat them, Cadbury Schweppes joined them in 1988 by licensing Hershey to manufacture and sell its chocolate products in the United States.

The company expanded its sugar confectionery product range in 2003 with the acquisition of Adams Confectionery from Pfizer Company, whose products include household brand names such as Certs mints, Halls cough drops, and Dentyne chewing gum.

Cadbury China

By the early 1990s, Cadbury Dairy Milk Chocolate was a well-established leading brand in Hong Kong, and throughout the 1980s the company was content to sell its products to China through Hong Kong's modern-day silk road. Inchcape JDH,

Ferrero's Hong Kong–based distributor, was Cadbury's distributor in Hong Kong for decades as well, and both chocolates shared the same gray-market distribution channel, though Cadbury in smaller volumes. Unlike Ferrero, which was satisfied with exporting its products to China indefinitely, in the early 1990s Cadbury believed it needed in-country manufacturing in order to achieve its goal of selling 1 billion chocolate bars there.

Mars, Cadbury's chief competitor in China, became the first of the Big Five chocolate companies to establish in-country chocolate manufacturing with the start-up of its Beijing factory in 1993. Cadbury reasoned that the longer Mars manufactured and sold its products in China, the more difficult Mars would be to beat in the competition for the affections of Chinese consumers. Cadbury was convinced that it had to make a decisive, significant move, and later that same year it began preparations to manufacture product in China as well.

Cadbury's manufacturing heritage and production technology was vested in its proprietary fresh-milk production process. Thus, the primary driver of its search for a suitable site for its factory was a local source of fresh milk. One location considered was Harbin, an inland city in the far northeast, near the Russian border. Harbin was the heart of one of China's main dairy regions—the same place Nestlé had selected for the location of its production facilities for powdered milk and infant formula. But locating the factory in remote Harbin would require Cadbury to deliver all of its perishable product over thousands of kilometers of China's antiquated transportation infrastructure that, at best, resembled that of the United States in the 1920s. China's chocolate markets were primarily retail stores in first-tier cities such as Beijing,

Shanghai, and Guangzhou, a great distance from Harbin. In addition, Harbin would be a difficult place to attract expat managers for multiyear assignments: winter temperatures were as low as −38 degrees Celsius (−36 degrees Fahrenheit).[3]

Cadbury eventually opted to locate its factory in suburban Beijing, which had a relatively well-developed infrastructure and is only half a day's drive from neighboring Tianjin's Xinggang Pacific seaport, which not only made exporting more cost-effective but also gave it the option to ship to southern China via sea freight, which was often more cost-effective and reliable than shipping overland in China. Though still 1,000 kilometers (621 miles) from the more developed retail environments in the relatively prosperous consumer markets of Shanghai and other large population clusters of eastern China, it was a far better choice than Harbin.

In October 1993, Cadbury Schweppes signed a joint-venture agreement with Beijing Farm Bureau, a state-owned company that controlled thirteen farms in and around Beijing that oversaw production of everything from wheat and corn to fruit and milk. The joint venture was named Beijing Cadbury Food Corporation, Limited (Beijing Cadbury), and was structured with an 85 percent Cadbury, 15 percent Beijing Farm Bureau equity holding between the two companies. A new factory was constructed from the ground up, with Cadbury contributing cash, equipment, and technical know-how, and Beijing Farm Bureau contributing the land. The joint venture was put under the supervision of Cadbury Australia Pacific Basin Region, owing to its proximity to China and familiarity with the region.

Though Beijing Farm Bureau's dairy farms' facilities were antiquated and their milk was of dubious quality and consistency, Cadbury gambled that it could be improved by the time the Beijing factory opened. Cadbury made a significant investment in these dairy farm operations, with piping, cleaning equipment, and a free supply of disinfectant to improve both the quality and hygiene of their milk. To further address hygiene concerns, Beijing Farm Bureau employed a fleet of trucks for daily raw-milk collection and delivery to a third-party facility, where the milk would be processed for use in chocolate making. Construction of the factory began in 1994 and equipment installation was completed in 1995.

Cadbury brought its manufacturing facility on line in stages by first importing large blocks of chocolate from Australia, then remelting and molding it into finished chocolate bars. This intermediate step allowed Cadbury to commission its molding and packaging equipment, train its new Chinese workers on the production machinery, and work the bugs out of its overall operation without having to actually make the chocolate itself—the most technically difficult part of the overall operation. By the end of 1995, Cadbury had stopped importing its chocolate and begun full-scale production at the Beijing factory.

Cadbury's China Morass

After the 1996–1997 chocolate season, an independent survey was conducted in first-tier cities that asked regular chocolate consumers two important questions. The first question was whether the consumer had ever eaten Dove or Cadbury chocolate. Approximately 90 percent responded that they had eaten both brands before. The second question was whether they had eaten Dove or Cadbury chocolate in the past six months. While nearly 90 percent had eaten Dove chocolate, only 5 percent reported eating Cadbury chocolate in the past six months. In spite of the improved competitive position its new in-country manufacturing operation provided, Cadbury was having difficulties developing among Chinese consumers a loyal following for its Dairy Milk Chocolate. One possible explanation for this counterintuitive phenomenon was the product's taste. The early China-made Cadbury chocolate had a cheesy smell that was also detectable in the product's taste. Cadbury Australia's quality assurance experts determined that the milk supplied to the factory was still of substandard quality and that the taste varied widely from source to source. Cadbury had lost its gamble that it could improve Beijing Farm Bureau's milk quality, and this had a profound adverse effect on the product's taste.

Having weaned Chinese chocolate consumers on the taste of its imported Australian-made chocolate during the 1980s and first half of the 1990s, Cadbury's paramount objective for its move to in-country manufacturing should have been to make the transition as seamless as possible for consumers. One option that would have virtually guaranteed Cadbury a smooth taste transition would have been to install a powdered-milk production process factory in China, and make the chocolate with Australian powdered milk. Cadbury's "a glass and a half of milk in every half pound of milk chocolate" slogan, combined with the image of milk pouring from two drinking glasses (one full and one half full) into a chocolate bar on the product's label, is one of the most successful and long-lived brand imaging campaigns of British advertising. The use of powdered milk rather than fresh milk would have in no way hindered Cadbury's ability to legally use this claim in China. However, this idea of using a powdered-milk process met significant resistance, since it required breaking with a century of worldwide success with its fresh-milk production process.

The fundamental reason behind Cadbury's decision to go with a fresh-milk production process, in spite of such glaringly apparent difficulties, was a pervasive dogmatic decision-making process toward establishing its business in China, which focused on replicating past successes rather than meeting the real-world challenges in China. This was apparent, for example, in the way Cadbury's industrial engineers designed the factory facility and production lines. They were technically comfortable and familiar with their proprietary fresh-milk technology and no doubt grappled with the lack of local chocolate-making machinery and maintenance suppliers on the ground in China. Under these circumstances, they instinctively fell back on their proven supplier base for fresh-milk production equipment when designing the factory, increasing the resistance to build a factory that used a different production process. As for the manufacturing department, keeping it simple and not reinventing the wheel by introducing a new production process would have been viewed as a prudent approach, particularly in a highly underdeveloped environment like China. Although all this made sense, and installing a fresh-milk factory was most salable internally, it did not address the real challenges the company would face in matching Cadbury Australia's chocolate taste using the fresh milk that was available in China.

Installing a fresh-milk factory ultimately burdened consumers with its technical problems in the form of product off-taste, which resulted in losing many of them altogether. Indeed, the decision to stick with fresh milk set in motion a commercial and administrative nightmare for Cadbury and ultimately cost it the opportunity to establish Cadbury Dairy Milk Chocolate as the preferred chocolate taste among China's first generation of chocolate consumers.

* * * * *

Aside from being better positioned to compete with Mars, Cadbury's decision to open a manufacturing plant in-country was justified by the fact that Cadbury Dairy Milk Chocolate bars were bought primarily for self-consumption. Thus, they offered a steadier, year-round business than gift chocolate, ensuring that a manufacturing plant would not be idle, and unproductive from a cost perspective, during much of the year. However, reliable statistics on chocolate consumption were difficult to find, and it was unclear to what degree purchases of chocolate for self-consumption were truly a year-round phenomenon.

Furthermore, there was no way to realistically estimate the true potential of China's evolving chocolate market because the country's transformation was occurring at blinding speed, and in every aspect of society: economic, political, and social. Long-range predictions were, therefore, inherently inaccurate. Yet such an estimate was critical, since key decisions about the size and scale of Cadbury's manufacturing investment depended on its market assessment. Thus, the key question for Cadbury was: How many Cadbury Dairy Milk Chocolate bars could be sold in China in the coming years and how quickly would the business grow? The answers would have to be based on best-estimate assumptions about the volume and frequency of consumption by the country's new chocolate consumers, the accessible populations of these consumers in major cities, and the growth of the chocolate market in general. Cadbury's assumptions in these areas, however, were founded on faulty reasoning.

Cadbury's overall business strategy for China was based on replicating the success of its Hong Kong and Singapore operations. Ferrero succeeded in replicating its Hong Kong business model in China because the company knew its product was a perfect fit for Chinese gift-giving expectations and did not need to be overly concerned about consumer consumption habits. Cadbury had a different challenge from Ferrero, though. Its chocolates were for self-consumption, and thus understanding and addressing Chinese consumption habits was essential.

Hong Kong and Singapore were prosperous and highly developed world-class cities that had well-established chocolate markets, and chocolate sales there were heavily influenced by large numbers of tourists and business travelers. Hong Kong had a population of 7 million, and 11 million visitors each year, most of whom hailed from countries with mature chocolate markets and brought their established chocolate habits (large volume and regular consumption) with them. During the factory-planning stages there was no effort by Cadbury to right-size its products for China through consumer research, and it modeled its China product range based on what was selling best in Hong Kong and Singapore, right down to package size and type. The assumption was that what sold there would sell in China.

Cadbury's star product in Hong Kong and Singapore was

its 250-gram (8.8-ounce) Dairy Milk Chocolate bar. In much smaller numbers, it was also its best seller, through Hong Kong's gray market, into China. But there was an element of self-fulfilling prophecy in this: it was Cadbury's best seller because that's primarily what Cadbury was shipping into China.

There was another bias at work, too: since larger chocolate bars move more efficiently through manufacturing facilities than smaller products, which require more packaging material per gram of chocolate and have the same production speeds,[4] basing projections primarily on the 250-gram (8.8-ounce) bar created more optimistic financial projections for Cadbury's future plant. In reality, a chocolate bar of this size was inappropriate for the consumption habits and disposable incomes of emerging Chinese consumers, who preferred to purchase chocolate in far smaller portion sizes. This meant that when the 250-gram (8.8-ounce) Cadbury Dairy Milk Chocolate bar and the 47-gram (1.7-ounce) Dove chocolate bar were side by side on the retail shelf, consumers had a much higher "investment risk" when trying Cadbury chocolate and were therefore more likely to pick up a Dove chocolate bar.

This fundamental forecasting mistake would come back to haunt Cadbury when its China factory opened, and it realized that it needed to right-size its products for Chinese consumers. Its best-selling sizes were the 45-gram (1.6-ounce) and 80-gram (2.8-ounce) bars, and when bagged bite-size chocolates began to command an increasingly significant portion of China's self-consumption market in the late 1990s, it would launch mini 12-gram (0.4-ounce) bars and even single-bite 6-gram (0.2-ounce) pieces. The result was that, even if the number of individual chocolate bars produced met produc-

tion forecast, the overall tonnage would be well below forecast, leaving the factory with a much larger chocolate-making
capacity than it actually needed.

Using Hong Kong and Singapore to develop a business
model for China also proved faulty, for another reason: both
had first-rate chilled distribution infrastructures, which
meant that distribution levels and sales volumes remained
fairly steady year-round. Assuming the same for China was a
miscalculation because it overlooked the fact that China did
not have a well-developed chilled distribution channel and
had relatively few air-conditioned retail stores. Overlooking
the extreme annual boom-and-bust seasonal fluctuations of
China's chocolate market led Cadbury to overplan its require-
ments for a market that was actually much smaller in size,
adding to its manufacturing capacity overestimation. After
the peak holiday season and the return of warm weather,
Cadbury's chilled supply chain wasn't well managed enough
to protect its product, and heat damage gave the product a
white mottled appearance.

Beijing Cadbury began feeling the impact of its overly optimistic sales projections that resulted in its carrying significant excess production capacity and consequently far too
much overhead cost. Having taken over the sales and distribution of its products in China from Inchcape JDH in 1994,
which was only effectively covering the cities of Beijing,
Shanghai, and Guangzhou, Beijing Cadbury's new sales organization succeeded in rolling out distribution of Cadbury
Dairy Milk Chocolate to ten additional cities by the 1996–
1997 season. However, the factory turned out far more product than Cadbury could sell, and average daily sales at the
retail level during the short peak season were far below expec-

tations, leaving huge stocks of unsold product clogging warehouses and retail shelves. Desperate to clear its aging stock, Cadbury began offering consumers two bars for the price of one, and even three for the price of one at the start of each chocolate season, in a last-ditch effort to clear the distribution pipeline to make way for new stock. The overstock problem caused the distribution and retail trade to lose confidence in Cadbury chocolate, dealing a serious blow to the company's brand image.

* * * * *

In the early 1990s, when Cadbury was contemplating an in-country manufacturing plant, it saw the lackluster performance of its Dairy Milk Chocolate bars as a function of its export business model. While exporting finished goods through Hong Kong's modern-day silk road worked in the short term, the chocolate maker was convinced that as long as its business was in the hands of others (distributors, traders, and wholesalers), it would consistently fall short of its potential. It reasoned that any enterprise serious about building its business must ultimately take control of the product's destiny, from in-country manufacturing through in-house sales and distribution management. Therefore, Cadbury believed that with the installation of its factory it would naturally follow that it would immediately take over sales, distribution, and collection for its products. Although this rationale was sound and worked for Cadbury elsewhere in the world, it ignored the reality that China's evolving distribution infrastructure was highly complex and that it would require a great deal of time and effort to establish a reliable chilled supply chain, vet new city distributors by trial and error, and build an effective in-house sales organization. These were all formidable challenges that few foreign companies, including Cadbury China, were prepared to meet.

When Cadbury opened its factory, China's commercial standards and practices were still at their early stage of transition from state-owned centrally planned structures to free-market structures, and in the absence of widely accepted commercial norms, personal relationships between the various links in the supply chain were key to establishing a working distribution system. China's commercial system, for example, lacked the kind of mechanisms that kept widespread defaults on payments in check in more developed economies. And the likelihood of getting paid diminished the farther away the sale was made from a company's home base—particularly if the sale were made across a provincial border. Accordingly, most multinationals insisted that their city distributors either make cash payment at the time of order (cash-on-order) or work through a national master distributor. Master distributors are larger, more established companies with multiple multinational clients, and thus are inherently more economically stable and reliable in terms of payment, since they have well-established relationships with city distributors and retailers across the country. Mars, for example, used a master national distributor during its start-up to great effect in China.

Assuming the distribution and sales functions itself, and discharging its in-country distributor, Inchcape JDH, added organizational complexity at a time when Cadbury could ill afford it. It could barely handle the challenge of fixing the product's taste, and concurrently building a first-rate sales, distribution, and collection organization in China became a significant burden. Moreover, the chocolate business in China was still hyperseasonal, even for self-consumption chocolate. Beijing Cadbury had a full-service, year-round manufacturing, sales, and distribution operation with all the attendant costs, but a highly seasonal retail business—and as a result, Cadbury began to hemorrhage money. Urgent action was needed, for the battle for the hearts, minds, and taste buds of China's first generation of chocolate consumers was being lost day by day.

Attempting to Turn the Tide

Cadbury China's first priority to get its business on track was to find a solution for the taste problem. Determined to stick with its fresh-milk process, rather than switch to imported milk powder, Cadbury's quality-control experts set out to fix the problem during the years 1996 to 1999 through additional control over both the milk sources and its processing. The operation became more selective in its sources of milk by paying a premium to acquire only the highest-quality milk, available from the three dairy farms.

On the processing side, Cadbury imported milking machinery to improve hygiene and cooling systems to better preserve the milk at the dairy farms so as to reduce the cheese flavor in the chocolate. Australia-based milk-processing experts would fly in six times a year to train the dairy farmers on the new equipment and how to properly use the disinfectant. Though it took several years and a relatively large amount of money, the effort paid off and the Beijing factory's chocolate finally met Cadbury standards for its Dairy Milk Chocolate. However, only time would tell if the country's chocolate consumers would forgive Cadbury for its misstep with the product's taste, and whether the company could effectively rebuild its standing with the distribution and retail trades.

It is sometimes said in business that strong sales cover many sins, and once committed to its China factory, Cadbury's only real option was to sell its way out of its overcapacity situation. One option for Beijing Cadbury to make use of its excess capacity was to develop export markets for its products. Though it managed to export specialty items to other Asian Pacific markets, such as gift boxes to Japan and drinking chocolate to Hong Kong and Australia, its export volume would remain relatively small and would not generate the kind of production volumes needed to significantly utilize the excess production capacity. The solution would need to come from within China and in the form of rapid domestic sales growth.

During the 1997–1998 chocolate season, Cadbury drew the line on geographic expansion at China's top twenty first-tier and second-tier cities, since the retail store quality and potential sales volume diminished significantly beyond these cities. The company focused on improving sales turnover in these cities and tailored its distribution and sales approach for the top three cities of Beijing, Shanghai, and Guangzhou.

For example, Beijing had relatively few large developed key accounts at the time, and as a northern city with four seasons, it offered a longer selling season in a large number of small non-air-conditioned retail outlets. Cadbury formed a small-store sales team that fanned out throughout the city to make direct sales to these retailers, while allowing a city distributor to supply its handful of Beijing key accounts.

By contrast, Shanghai's retail environment was dominated by large key accounts, such as Carrefour hypermarkets (superstores), the Huankelong and Jinkelong supermarket chain stores (which were rapidly approaching 1,000 outlets between them), and air-conditioned convenience stores. Small stores, such as non-air-conditioned mom-and-pop stores, constituted a relatively small portion of chocolate sales, since Shanghai's winters were both mild and short, effectively shortening their selling season. Cadbury, therefore, eliminated the use of distributors in Shanghai and formed its own sales team to make direct sales to the city's key account stores, with small stores taking care of themselves by purchasing what they needed off the wholesale market.

Because Guangzhou is in the subtropics, it presented significant fluctuations in seasonal distribution levels. The selling season in non-air-conditioned stores was extremely short—perhaps three months at best. However, the city had two things going for it: a strong cultural influence from nearby Hong Kong, where Cadbury was a household name, and its being one of the first major Chinese cities to economically benefit from China's experiments with special economic zones such as neighboring Shenzhen and Zhuhai. Consequently, it enjoyed one of the highest levels of prosperity and infrastructure development in China. Though Cadbury had far fewer key accounts here than in Shanghai, the city had a relatively well-developed chilled distribution and air-conditioned retail infrastructure, and the chocolate maker chose to make direct sales to its key accounts while letting local distributors handle the brief sales opportunity in small stores.

Cadbury eventually built an organization of approximately two hundred salespeople and merchandisers who covered these three key cities. Its customized distribution and sales solutions in these cities, along with its focus on the seventeen next best cities (using subdistributors), had a significant impact on growing its sales during the latter 1990s. But simply improving its chocolate's taste, as well as the corporation's sales and distribution, did not ensure Cadbury success in dominating China's chocolate market. Beijing Cadbury was not alone there, and its archrival Mars had not been idly standing by, waiting for Cadbury to get its act together.

The Battle for Chocolate Bars

At the end of the 1990s, as self-consumption of chocolate began to accelerate in China, Cadbury and Mars engaged in a heated head-to-head battle for the core self-consumption chocolate market segment—40-gram (1.4-ounce) to 80-gram (2.8-ounce) chocolate bars—with the main battlefield being the shelf space in retail stores for chocolate bars. Still grappling with its internal challenges and high overheads, Cadbury could ill afford what was essentially a spending war with Mars. And as a publicly held company incurring mounting losses in China, its parent company would not tolerate an indefinite war of attrition over the country's chocolate bar segment. Mars, on the other hand, was a family-owned company with deep pockets, and it was committed to prevailing, leaving Cadbury a limited window of opportunity to execute its come-from-behind sales initiative.

Having begun manufacturing and selling its Dove chocolate bars in China nearly three years before Cadbury, Mars was well prepared for battle. It led the market in media spending.

Its advertising slogan, "Silky smooth taste," effectively linked its brand with the chocolate mystique of self-indulgence that was growing among China's chocolate consumers, primarily by using television ads that targeted China's core chocolate consumers: emerging young urban professionals. Plus, Dove was produced with nearly all imported ingredients, including milk powder, and delivered on its promise of an indulgent chocolate experience. Not only did Cadbury's media spending lag behind that of Mars's, but for a while it used voice-over TV ads prepared for other markets, translating its "A glass and a half of milk in every half pound of milk chocolate" message to an uninspiring "Every 200 grams of milk chocolate contains a glass and a half of pure milk." Though informative, the ad simply did not resonate with Chinese consumers the way Dove's more emotional "Silky smooth taste" message did. One reason for this was that the Chinese were not frequent consumers of milk, making it difficult to visualize just how much milk was contained in a glass; was it a lot or a little? The image did little to help consumers identify with Cadbury chocolate or link its brand with a mystique of self-indulgence.

On the retail front, with its trademark competitive zeal, Mars aggressively exploited Cadbury's flavor fumble and distribution weakness by ensuring that its products always demonstrably dominated the retail shelf. With the resources of its national master distributor working for Mars, its chocolate was more consistently available than Cadbury's, and with good sales turnover, its product was fresher. Further, through the efforts of a dedicated team of in-store merchandisers, its product was better merchandised and became the focal point of China's chocolate retail shelves. During the peak season its displays were always the largest, best merchandised, and in the best locations. And when the peak season was over, Mars was first with aggressive stock-clearance programs to ensure a smooth transition into the off-season.

Cadbury got one thing right when planning its penetration of the China market: it knew that the longer Mars operated on the ground, the more effectively Mars would operate there, making it a formidable competitor. By the 2001–2002 chocolate season, Mars had significantly extended its lead in the chocolate market and Cadbury even lost its number-two market position to Hershey, an imported product with only a representative office in China, in the key market of Shanghai and a number of its prosperous satellite cities.

In a last-ditch effort to turn around its Dairy Milk Chocolate business, Cadbury developed a new milk chocolate formula designed specifically for the China market. In 2002, Beijing Cadbury converted to the new formula, which closely matched the taste and texture of Dove—effectively conceding the battle to establish its Dairy Milk Chocolate as the preferred chocolate taste among China's first generation of chocolate consumers. In spite of this desperate attempt to change the fortunes of its chocolate business, it was simply too little too late. Cadbury's chocolate business struggled to keep pace with China's rapidly growing chocolate market and remained only a market player, rather than market leader.

Though Cadbury's chocolate business in China may have been down, the company was not out of the confectionery market altogether. Its first China-made Cadbury Éclairs rolled off the production lines in 1996 and were quickly embraced by Chinese consumers. Individually wrapped bite-size sweets were a Chinese favorite, and Éclairs fit the mold.[5] They even found a niche within Chinese gift-giving traditions. It became fashionable, for example, for a bride and groom to give individual Éclairs gift boxes to their guests at wedding banquets.[6] By 2000, sales of Éclairs accounted for over half of the company's sales.

The success of Cadbury's Éclairs business and the 2003 Adams Confectionery acquisition was a boost to Cadbury's China business; Halls cough drops, for example, was a fairly well-established business in China that enjoyed good distribution and a solid consumer following at the time of the acquisition. Though these ancillary businesses were a financial shot in the arm for Cadbury China, and made an important contribution to keeping its doors open, they did little to contribute to Cadbury's Dairy Milk Chocolate business.

The Final Blow: A Breakdown of Leadership

Beijing Cadbury's first general manager headed the organization from 1993 to 1996. A career company man, he rose through the manufacturing ranks and presided over the factory start-up and switch to in-house sales and distribution. However, it would be Cadbury China's second general manager, who led the company from 1996 to 2001, who inherited the bulk of Beijing Cadbury's compounding operational and commercial problems. His subordinates describe him as having the leadership skills to deal with the myriad crises that came to a head during his tenure, most notably developing effective working relationships with Beijing Cadbury's variety of stakeholders, from factory workers and technical experts to its joint-venture partner and Chinese customers. Having worked through the technical fix of its chocolate's taste and having built Beijing Cadbury's national sales and distribution organization, he is credited with getting the major technical issues behind them. Though his leadership brought some hope and stability to the organization, it was not to last. After his departure, Cadbury China entered a chaotic phase in which its organization's leadership was perhaps more devastating to its fortunes in China than any of the operational or commercial crises that preceded it.

A new general manager took over the China organization in 2001, Cadbury China's third, but he stayed less than one year. He was followed by yet another general manager, whose strong marketing and sales background was hoped to aid in Beijing Cadbury's revitalization of its commercial operations, but this one left the organization within a year, in 2002, before he could make a substantial impact on the business. From 2002 to the end of 2004, Cadbury managed to hold a general manager in place for nearly two years, until Beijing Cadbury's first Chinese-speaking general manager, a Malaysian Chinese, came on board in 2005. With a stronger cultural connection than his predecessors, he took the reigns of the company with hard-driving sales manager–style leadership, but stayed less than two years. Ultimately, neither of these two managers had been successful, and Cadbury's Dairy Milk Chocolate business actually declined during their stewardship. In 2006, an interim manager from Cadbury India kept the general manager's seat warm until Beijing Cadbury's current general manager took over in 2007.

Before the company's current general manager, a total of six general managers—in as many years—had brought with them their own ideas as to how to turn Cadbury's Dairy Milk

Chocolate business around, but all failed. Moreover, the steady stream of new faces and continual shifting of strategic direction created an atmosphere of continuous instability within Beijing Cadbury, which had a detrimental effect on its organization's morale.

With the social chaos of the Cultural Revolution within living memory of many employees, there was universal disdain for this kind of disorder and the factional infighting that followed. Unlike the Cultural Revolution, however, Cadbury China's disaffected employees could vote with their feet, and the most effective and productive people left for greener pastures, while it became increasingly difficult to attract good people to the company. The impact of Cadbury's revolving-door leadership eventually became a full-blown crisis in and of itself. With its ineffectual leadership unable to provide a common vision for the business, the organization became increasingly inward focused, as employees grew more concerned about surviving the organizational chaos than about building its Dairy Milk Chocolate business with consumers.

* * * * *

While Cadbury was correct in assessing itself as one of the best positioned of the Big Five chocolate companies to dominate in China, from the day it opened its Beijing factory the entire operation became mired in internal issues and it strayed seriously off course from the primary task of building a following for its chocolate in China. Beijing Cadbury's revolving-door leadership demoralized the organization and its short-term leaders were unable to pull it together and successfully execute a recovery plan, if recovering its Dairy Milk

Chocolate business was even possible. Cadbury's distressed organization was simply unable to put forward a cohesive, competitive offense against Mars, and its chocolate business suffered as a result. By 2008, Cadbury's chocolate sales in China constituted only 0.5 percent of the company's total worldwide sales.[7] Selling a billion Cadbury Dairy Milk Chocolate bars, one to to each person in China, would remain an unachievable dream.

CHAPTER 4

Hershey

Back to Basics

There is a proverb about the owner of a shoe company in the early 1900s who, looking to expand into foreign markets, sent his most experienced salesperson on a clipper ship to Africa to explore new business opportunities. After a two-week journey and another week in country, the salesman sent a telegram saying, "ARRIVED SAFELY STOP PEOPLE HERE DON'T WEAR SHOES STOP NO BUSINESS STOP RETURNING NEXT SAILING." Undeterred, the owner of the shoe company then sent a much less experienced but highly motivated salesperson. After the long journey and a week in country he, too, sent a telegram, this one saying, "AR-

RIVED SAFELY STOP PEOPLE HERE DON'T WEAR SHOES STOP LOTS OF
BUSINESS STOP SEND HELP."

Hershey's early success in China can be attributed to a
fresh vision like the one of the inexperienced salesman of the
proverb. Hershey didn't have an entrenched international
business dogma to hold it back from meeting the challenges
of the future, especially in a country such as China, which was
undergoing fundamental change. Without a well-established
international business model to follow, Hershey's executives
had no choice but to rely on the fundamental principles of
their chocolate business in the United States to guide them in
China. They had to go back to basics. This would serve them
well in developing a low-risk, high-reward market-entry strategy and would, in fact, become a competitive advantage in
China's dynamic and evolving business environment.

The Hershey Company

Like its chocolate company rivals Ferrero, Cadbury, Nestlé, and
Mars, the Hershey Company is named after its founder, Milton
S. Hershey. Born in 1857, in rural Pennsylvania near where the
Hershey Company's headquarters is today, Milton Hershey had
a formal education that ended in the fourth grade, when he
became a printer's apprentice. Uninspired, a few years later he
took an apprenticeship at a Lancaster, Pennsylvania, confectionery shop and found his passion. At age nineteen Hershey
left Lancaster for Philadelphia, where in 1876 he started the
M.S. Hershey Wholesale and Retail Confectioner Company, but
the company failed six years later. Undeterred, by 1883 he was
back in business, now in New York City, but this venture failed,

too, as did another in Chicago. Hershey returned to Lancaster in 1886, broke but not broken. He quickly picked himself up once again and started the Lancaster Caramel Company, and he finally achieved the commercial success for which he had labored so long and hard.

Even this hard-won success, however, fell far short of Milton Hershey's true potential. In 1893, he attended the Chicago World's Fair,[1] where he would take a fateful first step that would lead to Milton Hershey's becoming the preeminent American chocolate maker: he purchased a chocolate-making machine. In 1894, he opened the Hershey Chocolate Company, and he began producing various chocolate products, including chocolate-covered caramels and baking chocolate. The business grew rapidly. Hershey sold Lancaster Caramel in 1900 and used the proceeds to construct a massive chocolate factory in Derry Township, Pennsylvania, the present-day Hershey, Pennsylvania, completed in 1905 and still in operation. Hershey's main products were the Hershey's Bar, which he launched in 1900, and Hershey's Kisses, launched in 1907. He brought Mr. Goodbar to market in 1925, Hershey's Syrup in 1926, chocolate chips in 1928, and Crackle in 1938. Hershey's chocolate had become an American institution.

Milton Hershey died, a legend, on October 13, 1945, one month after his eighty-eighth birthday, and he left behind a legacy as both an industrialist and a philanthropist. Hershey and his wife, Catherine, had created the Hershey Industrial School, an orphanage for boys in 1909, which was later renamed the Milton Hershey School. Widowed in 1915, and with no heirs to inherit his considerable wealth, Hershey donated nearly his entire fortune, including stock in the Hershey Company, to the Milton Hershey School Trust. The trust still holds over 30 percent of the stock and controls the majority of voting rights of the Hershey Company. In the latter part of his life, Hershey occupied himself with various philanthropic endeavors, and these values of giving back and commitment to community became an integral part of the company's culture.

From a business perspective, Hershey's legacy of dogged persistence and dedication to his dream paid off in ways that perhaps even he couldn't have imagined. The Hershey Company continued to grow well after his death as the company acquired Reese's Peanut Butter Cups in 1963, began producing KitKat for the U.S. market under license from the British chocolate maker Rowntree Products in 1969, and the company's product line grew to include nonchocolate candies such as Jolly Rancher chewy candies, Ice Breakers gum and mints, and BreathSavers mints.

Though the Hershey Company became an American icon, it was hardly alone in the marketplace and faced stiff competition from its main rival, the Mars family, whose products included powerhouse brands such as Milky Way, Snickers, and M&Ms. By the early 1970s, owing to competition from both Mars and others, Hershey's dominant share of the U.S. chocolate market began to erode. This prompted a twenty-year effort to regain its prominent position from its archrival Mars, largely through both internal growth and external acquisitions.

Hershey's International Business

Although Hershey succeeded in recapturing dominance of the U.S. chocolate market by the late 1980s, that success was the result of a near-total focus on the domestic market. Its business outside of North America amounted to less than 10 percent of total company sales. Furthermore, the company had limited capabilities in the international marketplace and none of its experiments with international business models were successful.

Hershey's dominance of the U.S. market, its unparalleled brand equity with American consumers, and its powerful domestic sales and distribution operation, when combined with the relative stability of that market, continued to overshadow opportunities in the global marketplace well into the 1990s. However, facing a mature and slow-growth chocolate market, the candy maker was compelled to look overseas for growth. It undertook major international initiatives in the 1990s following a pattern of trial and error such as that Milton Hershey had followed in establishing the Hershey Company itself.

While Hershey had an international division as far back as the 1970s, it was focused mainly on licensing, acquisitions, and joint ventures. The large and well-developed European chocolate market proved a difficult nut to crack, owing in large part to a negative perception of American chocolate. Europe's long and well-established chocolate tradition developed quite differently from that in the United States. For decades, the five-cent Hershey's Bar was at the center of the operation's marketing approach, bringing good-quality chocolate to the masses at an affordable price. This was so important to Hershey that it would resize the Hershey's Bar from time to time in response to changes in raw-material prices in order to maintain the five-cent value proposition for consumers. In contrast to Hershey's mass-market, mass-production approach, Europe's centuries-old chocolate tradition, rooted in its being an aristocratic indulgence, was founded on hand-made craftsmanship, high quality, and high prices to match. In spite of Switzerland's Nestlé and England's Cadbury having been among the first to industrialize the production of solid milk chocolate, Europeans still tended to look down on American chocolate as being too common, necessitating a long uphill battle for Hershey in Europe against well-entrenched preconceived notions about its chocolate. A popular slice of Hershey lore surrounds consumer response to Hershey's Kisses in a focus group conducted in Germany. Upon seeing a Hershey's Kiss dangling from the ribbon-shaped Hershey flag, some German consumers commented that it reminded them of a tampon.

An attempted acquisition of Swedish confectionery company Marabou in the early 1990s failed when Hershey lost out to a bid from Phillip Morris, which was seeking to further expand its already diverse portfolio of companies. The company tried to rebound from this high-profile acquisition failure with its so-called Patchwork Quilt Strategy for Europe, named after the patchwork quilts made by the Amish in communities that surround Hershey, Pennsylvania. The fundamental idea was that, through a series of strategic acquisitions of European chocolate and nonchocolate candy makers, Hershey would assemble a patchwork of capabilities, from manufacturing through sales organizations, throughout Europe that once knitted together would provide the organization with a strong overall competitive position in the European market. To that end, during the early 1990s, Hershey's successfully acquired Gubor Schokoladen in Germany, Sperlari Srl in Italy, and OZF Jamin in the Netherlands.

Gubor, which made premium boxed pralines and chocolates, had poor profitability that Hershey believed it could resolve through better management and incorporation into its European patchwork of companies. Only after Hershey bought the company did it realize that high costs built into the company's operating structure were not as easily worked out of the system as previously thought, owing in part to a substantial resistance to change within the Gubor organization. Gubor's irreparable high-cost operating structure did little to add to Hershey's competitiveness in Europe as once envisioned.

Sperlari was a sugar confectionery company with an internal sales force that was focused on distribution in the higher-end modern-trade channel (superstores, supermarkets, and convenience stores). However, sugar confectionery requires the broadest possible distribution in all channels, especially in the so-called down-trade channels (mom-and-pop stores, small neighborhood retail outlets, kiosks, etc.), to be successful in the long run. Without a distribution network that extended into the down-trade channel, there was little opportunity for Hershey to make inroads into the European confectionery market with the capabilities that the Sperlari acquisition offered.

OZF Jamin provided Hershey with contract manufacturing services, which Hershey envisioned as a producer of products for the emerging Eastern European market. But Hershey could make little practical use of OZF Jamin's production capacity. It simply didn't have the consumer base to justify the acquisition.

When Hershey divested all three of these European acquisitions in 1996, it served only to further negative perceptions within the organization regarding international expansion.

Europe was a bust, and it forced the company to look elsewhere if it were going to continue to explore foreign markets.
Hershey did achieve some success exporting American-made
product to Russia in the mid-1990s through a staging warehouse in Finland. The business grew rapidly and when it approached the $20 million annual sales threshold, Hershey
began preparations for establishing a manufacturing operation there. Eventually it would be the success of its export
business to Russia and failure of the OZF Jamin acquisition
that became the seed of the "build the business first, then
build the infrastructure" strategy that took root in Hershey's
international department in the mid-1990s.

In the spring of 1997, Hershey brought in an outsider to
become the new head of Hershey International. The hiring
was controversial because Hershey primarily promoted from
within when selecting leaders for its business. This new head
immediately took bold steps to give the international department its own identity, a strong sense of purpose, and a mandate for success. In the same way that IBM's mainframe
computer business once overshadowed its fledgling PC division in the 1980s, he believed that if the international team
remained at Hershey's headquarters, they would continue to
languish in the shadow of the domestic business and his international efforts would never gain the momentum they needed
to break free. One of his first actions was to convince Hershey's management to allow him to move the international
division out of Hershey, Pennsylvania—an unprecedented and
unpopular move within a company whose culture was so
deeply rooted in the theme-park environment of its hometown. South Florida was selected for the new international
office, since it provided easy access to Latin America, Her-

shey's largest export market at the time, and it was an ideal location for attracting international talent to the company.

The new International head intended to grow Hershey's international business through a distributor model, which focused on investing resources in marketing and distribution, rather than on fixed-asset investments such as a Russia factory. Within six months of his arrival he canceled plans for the Russia factory and Hershey effectively backed away from its business there. Shortly thereafter, Russia fell into a liquidity crisis, its economy imploded, and many foreign companies suffered huge losses. In hindsight, canceling plans for manufacturing in Russia was a good decision, at least in the short term.

Hershey China

At about the time of the new Hershey International head's arrival on the scene, an earlier international business development initiative was beginning to bear fruit. It was begun in late 1994, when Hershey created three teams to explore international business opportunities for its products. Each team comprised three functional experts—sales, logistics, and finance—and was assigned a geographic region: Eastern Europe, Latin America, or Asia. Hershey's missteps in Europe, and the chaotic transformation of former Soviet-block countries throughout the 1990s, were strong deterrents to anyone from Hershey recommending an aggressive business plan for Eastern Europe, and therefore the Eastern European initiative was dead in the water from the start.

The Latin America team put together a business plan that

culminated in the 2001 acquisition of the Brazilian brand Visconti and the formation of Hershey do Brazil. The Asia team saw big potential. Although Hershey had small export businesses to Asian countries such as Japan, Korea, and the Philippines, its biggest opportunity in the region was to start relatively fresh with consumers where it would not face a wall of preconceived ideas about its chocolate, the way it did in Europe. The challenge for Hershey was that Asia comprised an agglomeration of culturally unique countries at various stages of economic development, chocolate development, and Hershey's brand development, and therefore required unique business strategies for each country.

The individual selected specifically to lead Hershey into Asia was second-generation twenty-year Hershey veteran Todd Johnson (not his real name), the type of career employee whom Hershey people were fond of saying, "bleeds chocolate." He had a broad base of experience within the company, having worked in a variety of roles including marketing, finance, supply chain, and, for a time, as home-office marketing liaison for the Sperlari acquisition. Armed with a deep understanding of the fundamentals of the chocolate business, he traveled throughout Asia conducting basic market research and talking with anyone who would talk to him—even the competition.

Initial countries of interest were Indonesia, India, and China. Indonesia made the list because of its relatively large population, but it quickly dropped off the list because it is an archipelago of tropical islands with an underdeveloped distribution infrastructure. Maintaining product quality throughout the supply chain would be too difficult.

India was promising because it is the world's second most

populous country, with a large and growing middle class. India also had a strong chocolate heritage as a result of centuries of British colonial influence. India's chocolate market was estimated at $100 million in the mid-1990s, with Cadbury holding about an 80 percent market share. Johnson knew that Hershey would face serious competition, and he identified a number of major barriers for Hershey in India, especially the state of the country's distribution infrastructure. India's lack of an air-conditioned supply chain and air-conditioned retail stores meant that, to an Indian, chocolate was a half-melted Cadbury bar.

In addition to India's infrastructure challenges, its class system ensured that those who could afford chocolate had domestic employees do much of the daily shopping. Since most chocolate around the world is purchased on impulse (e.g., grabbing a chocolate bar off the rack while waiting at the supermarket checkout), these domestic employees constituted a barrier to sales, inasmuch as they are sent to the supermarket to buy what is on their employer's shopping list and are unlikely to decide on their own that their employer might suddenly have a craving for chocolate. With domestic employees acting as gatekeepers between Hershey and the ultimate consumer, Hershey's in-store promotion and merchandising efforts to drive brand switching from Cadbury would be ineffective. And, even if Hershey got past consumers' domestic employees, the company would then need to overcome the consumers' well-established taste preference for Cadbury chocolate. Finally, India's complicated import processes and high import duties made it an even less attractive option.

Johnson concluded that, since there was lower-hanging fruit to be had in other markets in Asia, rather than tackle

India's formidable infrastructure problems, Hershey would focus its resources on building its brand with consumers in more readily accessible markets. The Philippines offered Hershey the opportunity to build upon the business it had already established with Filipino consumers who often shopped at retail stores on American military bases, most notably Subic Bay Naval Base and Clark Air Base. In addition, Duty Free Philippines, a retailer that targeted international travelers, was virtually a market of its own. It offered access to a captive audience of millions of Filipino workers as they passed through Philippine airports, with cash in their pockets, traveling to and from places of work around the world.[2] Johnson identified Duty Free Philippines as a priority, and it became such an important submarket to Hershey International that it earned its own line-item status on company sales reports. Likewise, Japan and South Korea, by virtue of hosting U.S military bases, offered opportunities for further development. China, however, remained a tantalizing enigma and demanded a special approach.

* * * * *

The China market was difficult to get a handle on in the 1990s. Basic information about the chocolate market there, such as annual volume turnover, qualified distributors, demographic statistics, and the number and location of retail outlets, was difficult to access, if it existed at all. In addition, China's ever-changing maze of bureaucratic rules and regulations further contributed to the uncertainty. China had no chocolate tradition, a population of mostly inaccessible consumers who had little disposable pocket money for a luxury like chocolate, and an underdeveloped distribution infrastructure that, like India's, presented a huge challenge in ensuring that product arrived in front of consumers in reasonable shape.

As part of his due diligence, Johnson arranged formal interviews with bankers, logistics companies, manufacturers, and distributors to develop an understanding of the China opportunity and to devise a broad-stroke route to market for Hershey's products. He even managed to get invited to Wrigley's China plant in 1994 and toured the facility of local chocolate manufacturer Le Conte.[3] He also learned a great deal from informal hotel bar and lobby conversations with representatives of other companies who were doing similar due diligence, or who were in the process of establishing representative offices and operations in China. In the end, he was convinced that the potential for Hershey to establish its chocolate products with the growing number of accessible Chinese consumers merited a proactive, if pragmatic approach.

One of Johnson's missions was to determine whether manufacturing Hershey products in China was essential to Hershey success there and, if so, to vet options for doing so. Johnson became aware that Cadbury's China factory was running at about half its production capacity and incurring relatively high fixed costs as a result. One in-country manufacturing option considered was to simply work out an arrangement with Cadbury to utilize its spare capacity. However, in spite of a long-established licensing arrangement between Cadbury and Hershey in the U.S. market,[4] having Cadbury produce Hershey products in China was not salable internally, since Hershey management was wary about losing consistency in its products if produced by third parties. Given Cadbury's struggles with its own product quality during its first few years producing chocolate in China, this turned out to be prudent.

Two aspects of the Chinese chocolate market were instrumental in Johnson's decision about manufacturing Hershey chocolate in China. First was the high retail price for chocolate in China, attributable in large part to Mars and Cadbury having established factories there. High prices were necessary to pay back the investment made in these factories. This served as a financial umbrella under which Hershey could sell imported products in China at a relatively high price, and it was a stabilizing factor for chocolate retail prices, since these investment burdens for Hershey's competitors would not go away overnight. Second was the relatively low cost of exporting finished goods from Hershey's North American factories. China's import duty for imported chocolate was then only 12 percent. Combined with a 3 percent cost of ocean freight from the U.S. to China, selling U.S.-made product in China cost only 15 percent more than selling it in the United States. Johnson determined that more than acceptable gross margins could be achieved by exporting finished goods from Hershey's existing factories—enough even to support a respectable amount of consumer marketing investment. While temporarily exporting to a country to seed the market for future development is not a unique idea (many companies followed the very same strategy to great effect), with competitors Cadbury, Nestlé, and Mars already manufacturing in-country, it was getting late in the game: a decision had to be made.

Johnson concluded that Hershey did not need to manufacture its products in China to build a business there, which fit perfectly with the company's "build the business first, then build the infrastructure" international business development approach. In making his recommendation to Hershey, Johnson explained that information was scarce and admitted that the opportunity was therefore difficult to quantify. Nevertheless, he insisted that China was too significant a market to dismiss. He recommended that Hershey test the waters and let the business evolve along with the development of China's chocolate market. He also recommended that the company not make an initial investment in manufacturing. This not only would prove prescient, it was also critical to selling Johnson's proposal to Hershey's management, especially given the company's less than stellar international track record. With investment risk minimized to appease even the most risk-averse decision makers in the company, he was given the go-ahead to proceed with the China test-market. This approach would pay substantial dividends far down the road and in ways unforeseen at the time.

* * * * *

With his China test-marketing plan authorized, Johnson's next step was to develop an operating framework for bringing Hershey's products to market in China. He was convinced that the China test-market required some form of permanent presence on the ground and he chose the representative office as Hershey's initial legal entity structure in China. The Chinese government recognized that companies needed time to conduct basic market research, make distributor and customer contacts, and sort out entry strategies, and so it had authorized representative offices as a vehicle for doing so. Like Ferrero, Hershey needed an importer to bring the product into the country and a distributor to get the product through China's antiquated supply chain and make it available within the "arc of the reach" of Chinese consumers.

One option for doing both was to follow the Ferrero model and employ a full-service third-party logistics (3PL) company to provide turnkey import, sales, distribution, and collection services. A search for 3PL companies with the right capabilities led Johnson to his preferred choice, Hong Kong–based SIMS Trading, but SIMS had a conflict of interest: It had a distribution relationship with Nestlé, one of Hershey's direct competitors.[5] Hershey was forced to go with its second choice, which in the interest of confidentiality will hereafter be referred to as "Second Choice." With a 3PL company managing the physical distribution and collection side of the equation, the main role of Hershey's representative office would be to monitor the 3PL company, guide implementation of strategy, and conduct market research and brand development activities.

The next decision was where to locate Hershey's representative office. Cadbury, Nestlé, and Mars had all established their China manufacturing operations in or near Beijing in the north. Southern China offered the distribution infrastructure of the modern-day silk road, which brought Ferrero Rocher to market in China. But Johnson was reluctant to establish Hershey's operations in Beijing, since it was still emerging from its time warp of monolithic central planning and ossified bureaucracy, and had no intention of having Hershey enter the fray of the chaotic gray-market channels of southern China.

There was, however, an option in eastern China that offered a middle ground, literally and figuratively, between the two. With Hershey's "build the business first" strategy well in mind, Johnson chose to locate the representative office where the most geographically, financially, and culturally accessible consumers were—Shanghai. In addition to meeting all three of these criteria, Shanghai offered many other advantages. Although difficult to measure, Shanghai had an "open for business" environment and was a preferred place to station an expatriate who would be staffing the office. Further, it had a population of 19 million people and enjoyed a provincial-level status, effectively removing one layer of the city-provincial-national government bureaucratic hierarchy. Shanghai is also at the heart of the Yangtze River Delta region of China, a cluster of relatively prosperous cities located in eastern China that includes Nanjing, Hangzhou, and Suzhou. This proximity offered the potential for rapidly developing the region surrounding Shanghai, since market-development efforts in Shanghai would likely spill over into these neighboring cities. Shanghai's distribution infrastructure was also among the most developed in China, from having a modern ocean port to having more air-conditioned retail stores than in all of northern China combined. But most important, Shanghai residents had one of the highest disposable income levels of any major city in China and were accustomed to foreign products and concepts on a level rivaling even the heavily Hong Kong–influenced people of Guangzhou (the capital city of Guangdong Province) and Shenzhen.

With the operating structure analysis behind him, Johnson faced the most important and onerous decision for any international business manager: selecting the right person to lead an in-country operation. The ideal person would be someone who had both industry and China experience. However, because chocolate was relatively new to China, for all intents and purposes this person did not exist. So, like other managers setting up business operations in China at the time, he had to choose between someone from within the company with the chocolate-industry experience and someone from outside the company with China experience. He chose the former, believing that understanding the fundamentals of the chocolate business was of paramount importance for success in China. Further, bringing someone from within Hershey to run the China operation would at least ensure transplantation of the company culture. That person would also have immediate credibility within Hershey, making it easier for Johnson to garner internal support for the China initiative. For example, Hershey's North American plants would probably be more willing to accommodate special requests—say, for a small production or specialty run designed especially for the China market—if that request came from someone they already knew and respected. Justifying 20 to 30 percent salary increases for Hershey China employees—not uncommon at the time since Hershey needed to compete with the likes of P&G and Nestlé for the same limited pool of Chinese executives— would meet less resistance if coming from a trusted Hershey insider than from a new manager hired from outside the company. Finally, he understood that while China experience was certainly valuable, as China transformed its economy, a leader with the right personal characteristics, a tolerance for ambiguity, and the ability to deal with continuous change would be sufficient to address the China side of the equation.

Johnson's search led him to Tim Porter (not his real name), another twenty-year Hershey veteran who offered a well-rounded general management background within the company. Porter had a reputation for exceptional personal discipline and a systematic professional approach to his work, which Johnson believed were the characteristics that would serve the company well in China's mercurial business environment. Johnson's next challenge was to convince Porter not only to move his family halfway around the world to a developing country (Porter had never been outside of North America), but also to depart the coveted and successful domestic business operation to assume a test-marketing exercise within Hershey's battered International division. The assignment was pitched as a three-year mandate to study the market through a test launch of Hershey products in Shanghai, create a sustainable business model, and subsequently roll out to additional cities. This assignment initiated an exemplary working relationship between Johnson at the head office and Porter at the China office that, based on trust and mutual respect, would provide stability and continuity to Hershey's efforts in China, and prove to be a competitive advantage.

The First Season: 1995–1996

Most expatriate assignments fail because employees and their families are unable to adapt to their new environment, and from the very start, the Porter family would face many challenges adjusting to their new life in China. When they moved to Shanghai in the summer of 1995, on their way from the airport to the crowded city, their taxi stopped at an intersection where they saw people sitting on stools along the median of the road, their pant legs rolled up over their calves and their shirts rolled up over their midsections, fanning themselves to keep cool in the summer heat. China was literally, and figuratively, a world away from the well-manicured and picturesque Hershey, Pennsylvania, they knew and loved.

In addition to culture shock, the inability to communicate in the local language proved a constant challenge for daily activities like banking, taking taxies, and grocery shopping. In spite of these difficulties, the Porter family took it all as a great learning experience, were committed to making it work, and eventually settled into the expatriate lifestyle in Shanghai. Johnson had chosen well.

Porter's first task was to convert Johnson's basic business model into an operating plan for the China market test. His first step was to define the basic marketing mix, or classic 4Ps of marketing: product, price, place (distribution), and promotion.

Retail chocolate shelves in China were generally divided into two distinct sections: the chocolate bar section and the chocolate gift section. The chocolate bar section comprised Mars's Dove bars and Cadbury bars ranging in size from 40 grams (1.4 ounces) up to 250 grams (8.8 ounces). With only chocolate bars available on the retail shelf, and nothing to indicate anything to the contrary, it was reasonable to assume that for self-consumption purposes, Chinese consumers preferred to buy their chocolate in bars.

The decision was made to launch with four products: the Hershey's Bar, the Hershey's Bar with Almonds, Hershey's Kisses, and Hershey's Kisses with Almonds, all Hershey institutions. Following the market leaders, the flagship product in China would be the Hershey's Bar, with its label's large and prominent "HERSHEY'S" brand acting as an on-shelf billboard. But which of Hershey's variety of chocolate formulas would best suit the taste preferences of Chinese consumers and thus be the most effective in a head-to-head competition with Cadbury and Mars for dominance of the chocolate bar section? Porter conducted a consumer taste preference test of nine Hershey chocolate formulas, from Hershey's Special Dark, which was on the bitter side, to sweet and creamy Hershey's Symphony chocolate. Hershey's extra creamy formula was most preferred of the nine formulas and was launched in China.[6] The point was to put the consumer at the forefront of product selection.

Because Hershey arrived in China a few years after its major competitors, it had less room to maneuver in setting a price on its products. It had three pricing options: premium, parity, or discount pricing versus the market leaders, Cadbury and Dove.[7] Distributors and salespeople invariably argued that "cheaper is easier to sell," and, indeed, discount pricing seemed logical in a country where few consumers, at that time, had any disposable income. But there were other considerations. Chinese consumers were, and are, extremely brand conscious and are often willing to pay exorbitant prices for the prestige of being associated with top brands. Having lived with inferior quality for most of their lives, people naturally wanted the best if they could obtain it, even if it meant paying a substantial premium. And, since Chinese consumers had little experience with chocolate, their choices were guided almost entirely by brand awareness, packaging, and pricing.

If Hershey adopted a discount pricing strategy, it would run the risk that Chinese consumers would conclude its chocolates were inferior. How, they might ask, can Hershey's chocolate, which is made in the United States and imported, be cheaper than Dove, which is made in China, unless it's a substandard product? Could it be a local copy-product? So, despite the advice of his local distributors and salespeople, and warnings of failure if Hershey didn't bargain-price, Porter decided to launch at prices comparable to Dove's. Sales took off and Hershey never looked back.

As for place, "follow the air-conditioning" was the key determining factor for the selection of target retail outlets. This was necessary for a chocolate product, but it had the added advantage of allowing Hershey to follow the money, since air-conditioning was a feature typically found in retail stores with the highest average sales per customer in China. The downside of this "follow the air-conditioning" strategy was that, even on a national level, these stores numbered around 3,000 outlets at the time, with nearly half located in Shanghai.[8] Although small neighborhood markets, mom-and-pop stores, and kiosks were vastly more common, the absence of air-conditioning meant they were seasonal distribution opportunities at best. Further, their open-to-the-street storefronts in China's major cities like Shanghai, which were undergoing major infrastructure construction projects, inundated them with dust. Keeping the product presentable for consumers in these stores would be a constant problem.

On the product promotion front, rolled-up pant legs and people fanning themselves by the roadside notwithstanding, Porter's first real culture shock after arriving in China was the complete lack of awareness of the Hershey brand among distributors, retailers, and consumers. For a career Hershey employee accustomed to nearly universal brand awareness among American consumers, this was a shock. But it was also an opportunity to write on a clean slate and to get it right with Chinese consumers.

Porter opted for an educational approach toward Hershey's consumer communication platform in China. He wanted to create awareness of the company's century-long legacy in the States (including the story of Hershey's founder), and even educate consumers about what chocolate is. Television was the most effective medium for communicating these messages, and it was where Hershey's competitors were advertising, too. More important, for the Chinese consumer, television gave brands credibility.

A television advertisement needed to be created from scratch because Hershey had not needed to communicate who Milton Hershey was and what a Hershey's Bar is to American consumers since well before the advent of television, and therefore no such ad existed. A nostalgic-style ad featuring turn-of-the-nineteenth-century images of Milton Hershey, old-style chocolate making, and the Hershey's Bar was created specifically for the China market.

In the mid-1990s, chocolate consumers were a tiny percentage of the population. They were scattered in cities spread over a large geographic area and had few retail outlets where they could buy the product. It was critical, then, that advertising and promotions be highly targeted. For example, offering free samples to consumers would take place primarily in retail stores that already carried the chocolate. This not only ensured that Hershey was reaching consumers who had access to Hershey's products but it also linked promotional spending directly to sales. Other promotional events, outside of stores, were designed to build brand awareness, both at the promotional event and through media coverage of it. For example, on a busy Sunday afternoon on the Bund, a popular riverfront boulevard in central Shanghai, a local celebrity was hired by Hershey to attract passers-by who would receive Hershey's chocolate samples on the spot. The promotional theme of the event was to raise money for local orphanages, a direct link to Hershey's roots with the Milton Hershey School.

The fact that Hershey's products were imported from the United States was a promotional advantage because Mars, Cadbury, and Nestlé products were all manufactured in China. Hershey exploited the Chinese perception that imported products are of higher value by prominently displaying "Made in the USA" on both packaging and promotional materials.

A fifth, and perhaps the most important "P" for Porter to address, was people. In the mid-1990s, finding and retaining experienced local employees was difficult in China. A vestige of the country's command economy was that students rarely chose their fields of study—they were assigned. So job applicants for sales and marketing positions, for example, would often have degrees in engineering or sciences and unrelated work experience with state-owned organizations, to which they were also assigned, that had operating principles and practices that had little in common with those of multinational companies. This complicated the already daunting challenge of building an effective multifunctional team in China.

Unable to find applicants who had the qualifications specified on job descriptions, Porter had to look for personal qualities that would provide a good foundation for professional skill development. He took an unusual approach to hiring, often conducting interviews not in his office but in retail stores with chocolate shelves. Instead of asking applicants to tell him about themselves, he would often begin by asking them to tell him about the shelf in front of them. How they handled such a question would reveal a lot about their self-confidence, commercial common sense, and desire to learn. Once hired, Porter often found his employees had solid negotiating skills that were enhanced by their local knowledge and familiarity with Chinese cultural norms. Indeed, despite their inexperience and lack of formal training, many simply by virtue of being bright and Chinese turned out to be more effective negotiators than experienced expatriates. Porter also found that his local employees were happy to work long hours and were eager to capitalize on the opportunity for professional development within a multinational company. Further, they enjoyed the air-conditioning in summer and heat in the winter. The office was generally more comfortable than home.

Another challenge for Porter was to develop an effective leadership style for directing and motivating his young team. This was especially tricky because almost all of his staff had worked for state-owned companies with a top-down management style. Employee initiative was not encouraged or rewarded; workers looked to their bosses for constant direction and rarely took risks. Porter knew that there was a big adjustment in the offing, but he wanted to bring his new staff along gradually by establishing a mentor-student relationship with them, where they were challenged to think, expected to offer ideas, and encouraged to take a hands-on approach to learning. His small team valued the kind of work environment that made them part of the management of the operation rather than simply executers, and this served to further enhance the loyalty of his staff. Though many were offered higher pay by other multinational companies in China, they tended to stay with Hershey. This paid dividends in the form of strong personal relationships with people working in the distribution and retail end of the business. In a relationship-based culture like China, strong business relationships result in strong sales, and therefore these relationships became an important factor in Hershey's China success.

Armed with a 5Ps framework and a couple of ocean shipping containers of chocolate, in the fall of 1995, Porter and his young China team began test-marketing Hershey's products with Chinese consumers in selected Shanghai retail stores. Sales were good and consumer feedback was positive, and all indications were that Hershey's chocolates were able to make a connection with Chinese consumers. But many more questions remained to be answered if Hershey was to succeed in its new commitment to build a business development model for a national rollout of its products in the world's fastest-growing consumer market.

The Second Season: 1996–1997

Based on things learned during the first test-market season in China, Hershey would undertake several important refinements in its business model and marketing mix during the second season, beginning with its fifth P. By the second season, Porter felt that he had not succeeded in forging a shared vision with his local staff of the total business he was building in China, from placing orders to Hershey's factories in the United States through in-store merchandising in Shanghai's retail stores. In 1997, to help communicate his vision of the business, he took some of his local staff to the Philippines to see firsthand Hershey's successful operation there. They spent several days speaking with the company's Philippines employees, who explained their jobs and work processes; walking through distributor warehouses; and visiting as many retail stores as they could before their flight home. The trip accomplished two things: it got the team moving toward a common vision of the business and it instilled a sense of loyalty and commitment to the company, since international travel was a source of prestige for Chinese people.

Packaging was next on the list. In the 1990s, Hershey International had developed generic international packaging in an attempt to create a one-size-fits-all design that would not offend people from cultures as diverse as the Middle East and Japan. The packaging was beige, and while it did not offend consumers everywhere, it did not excite them, either. Further, Hershey adopted an over-brand strategy, which is to market multiple products under a single master brand name, rather than spending more money advertising and promoting multiple brands. For example, instead of promoting both the Hershey's brand and the PayDay brand, the name of PayDay was replaced with a generic description: Hershey's Peanut Caramel Bar. This didn't fly with consumers, however, and therefore the timing was right to obtain authorization for Hershey China to go its own way with packaging design. It was an opportunity for the company to adopt gold as the Hershey China color for self-consumption chocolate.[9] Like Ferrero Rocher, gold was an ideal choice, since it advertised premium quality and good fortune to Chinese consumers—just what Hershey China wanted to communicate through its packaging.

Porter also revisited the decision to use a full-service 3PL company, and he concluded that they were too expensive. They operated on high margins relative to their costs, had superficial market penetration, and for the most part used local distributors to execute physical distribution and collection activities. Second Choice had limited core competency in physical distribution in China, making its value as an intermediary questionable. Porter even suspected that it intended to use Hershey's business to develop its distribution capabilities, but even that was not being satisfactorily accomplished. So, by the start of the 1996–1997 season, Hershey engaged a so-called master distributor, Shanghai Shanlong, to bring its products into China on a cost-plus basis and to resell them to city distributors. Shanghai Shanlong was already acting as master distributor of imported Japanese confectionery products in China, so it seemed a natural fit. Hershey's representative office would continue to closely monitor the implementation of Shanghai Shanlong (which Porter termed "Shadow Management"), and his China team would continue to focus on all aspects of product marketing.

Porter extended his test-marketing exercise to four satellite cities of Shanghai: Wuxi, Suzhou, Ningbo, and Hangzhou. Selected for their demographic similarity, the launches in Wuxi and Suzhou were used to test effective levels of advertising and promotion. In Wuxi, Hershey withheld television advertising but provided in-store promotion support in the form of point-of-sale merchandising and sampling. In Suzhou, Hershey launched a television media campaign, but with little or no in-store promotion support. By comparing the peak-season sales results, this experiment provided valuable data for fine-tuning the marketing mix and establishing minimum advertising and promotion levels for launching into new cities.

The results of Hershey's second test-marketing season provided this kind of essential information that allowed Porter to refine its marketing mix into an investment formula for launching the company's products to new cities with effective levels of advertising and promotional support, which ensured strong sales and a successful launch. Most important, it led to a discovery that sparked Hershey's rapid ascent as a viable player in China's first-tier city chocolate market.

* * * * *

The fact that the two leading chocolate companies in China at the time, Cadbury and Mars, were selling chocolate bars was the primary reason Hershey chose to lead with its own venerable Hershey's Bar. However, it quickly became evident that Hershey's Kisses offered some point of difference that was meaningful to Chinese consumers, since the sales of Hershey's Kisses far outpaced those of Hershey's Bars. Like Ferrero Rocher, Hershey's Kisses have an appeal that transcends cultures (some German consumers excepted). Nobody knows for sure how Kisses acquired its name, but the conventional wisdom is that someone once remarked that the chocolate production machinery emitted a kissing sound when making the product, and the name stuck. Hershey's Kisses had a cuteness in their shape—in particular the roundedness of their bottom edge that some consumers have fondly likened to the shape of a baby's bottom that appealed to consumers—but the main attraction was that Hershey's Kisses offered consumers a bite-size portion of chocolate.

It was discovered that Kisses' cute and whimsical nature connected on an emotional level with Chinese chocolate consumers, just as it did with Americans. However, the bigger discovery was that Chinese consumers' purchase behavior was significantly different from their consumption behavior. Although Chinese consumers purchased 40-gram (1.4-ounce) and larger bars because that was what was on the retail shelf, they generally consumed far less whenever they actually ate chocolate, perhaps only 10 to 20 grams (0.35 to 0.7 ounces) per occasion. With the average Hershey's Kiss weighing between 4 and 5 grams (about 0.15 ounces), three or four Kisses were just about the right snacking portion for most Chinese consumers.

Sharing also proved to be a key facet of Chinese chocolate consumption behavior, which aided consumers' acceptance of Kisses. Chocolate bars are a clumsy and unhygienic format for use over multiple eating occasions. They are difficult to protect once the seal is broken and require consumers to touch the chocolate with their mouths or fingers when attempting to eat smaller portions, making sharing that much more difficult. Food safety and hygiene is a pervasive problem in China, and this plays a role in how Chinese consumers handle food products—touching food with one's hands is generally not well accepted. A bag of individually wrapped Hershey's Kisses offered a convenient and hygienic format for both consuming and sharing, and individually wrapped confections were a traditional and familiar packaging format for local Chinese sweets, such as China's White Rabbit candy. That a product created for American consumers in 1907 had relevance and made the same powerful connection with Chinese consumers in 1997 demonstrated that great ideas are both universal and timeless.

The beauty of Hershey's "build the business first, then build the infrastructure" strategy was the flexibility to capitalize immediately on the bite-size discovery, which it did. Had the company invested millions of dollars in a chocolate bar production line in China, the pressure would have been to keep the line running—whether consumers wanted more bars or not—thus inhibiting its ability to capitalize on the popularity of Kisses. Short-term decision making and corrective measures to cope with lack of demand for bars would have been the order of the day. With no commitment to plant and equipment in China, Porter simply ordered fewer Hershey's Bars and more Kisses from Hershey's North American factories. This change in product focus would not be without some cost, though, since Hershey's TV advertisement and promotional materials would need to reflect the new emphasis on Hershey's Kisses.

There were three options available for the development of a new television ad. The "Milton Hershey/100 Years" message could be adapted to Hershey's Kisses, an entirely new ad could be created, or an existing U.S. ad could be used with a Chinese language voice-over. Consistent with Hershey's overall approach to the China market, consumers were asked what they preferred through advertising concept tests. Hershey had long promoted Kisses' cute and whimsical qualities through its "Little Hershey's Kiss, Big Chocolate Taste" ad campaign, which was very successful in the U.S. market. Since Chinese consumers had already accepted Kisses' taste, shape, and size, it was not surprising that this ad resonated best with Chinese consumers as well. The campaign offered Hershey the opportunity to shift gears to an advertisement that was far more entertaining in its approach to educating consumers about Hershey's chocolate; focused Hershey's core consumer message on taste, which was ideal for a taste-driven product category like chocolate; and, as it would be discovered years later, was highly memorable.

After only two seasons in China, copy Kisses were popping up in the Shanghai market. Porter was shocked not only at the speed with which Hershey's Kisses were copied but also at the delight of his staff that the product was being copied at all. Naturally, given China's lack of historical development of intellectual property rights, they saw it as a sign of Hershey's success in Shanghai and just another feature of the country's emerging capitalist economy. Like Ferrero, Hershey didn't see it that way. Having wisely trademarked the Kisses' two-dimensional shape (its silhouette profile), it had the legal basis to vigorously enforce trademark rights against any product that resembled a Hershey's Kiss. Therefore, unlike Ferrero Rocher, the copying of Hershey's Kisses remained only a minor nuisance.

The Third, Fourth, and Fifth Seasons: 1997–2000

By the company's third season in China, its business was beginning to generate momentum and its local management team members were beginning to find their footing in their new jobs. It was time to put Hershey's business model, refined during its first two seasons, to the test by breaking out of the eastern region of the country and rolling out to two additional cities: Guangzhou to the south and Beijing to the north. Hershey's product launch in Beijing was also a psychological thrust into the heartland of competitors Mars, Cadbury, and Nestlé. The sentiment among the China team was that if Hershey could make it in Beijing, it could make it anywhere in China.

The launches in Guangzhou and Beijing were successful

since Hershey's products were well received by both distributors and retailers, eagerly accepted by consumers, and sales met expectations. This achievement was due in large part to Hershey China's well-balanced marketing mix, but also to Porter's penchant for discipline, which proved to be an important asset when rolling distribution out to more geographic areas, since it succeeded in bringing a degree of control within China's complex and often perplexing distribution system. Hershey steered clear of common pitfalls that have bedeviled many multinational companies in China. For example, at a trade show in Shanghai, a distributor from Harbin, a city in the far northeast of China, tried to place a relatively large order for Kisses on the spot but was politely refused. Hershey's budget and sales plan was fixed for the coming season and could not provide adequate marketing support in Harbin. The distributor insisted he would worry about that. But without adequate support, Hershey's brand would be tarnished if the product failed to move off retail shelves. Porter held his ground, resisting the temptation for a quick sales boost by launching products in any city without adequate marketing support. Hershey's reputation as a consistently good seller remained intact.

As the test-marketing exercise continued to unfold, Hershey's China operation was under considerable pressure from the home office to rapidly accelerate its sales and distribution rollout and become a fully operational profit center for Hershey International. Indeed, this was a major source of friction between Porter and the new head of Hershey International. But Porter was determined not to overreach the achievable opportunity in China. In this he found a staunch ally in Johnson, his boss and advocate at the international headquarters.

A colonial-era British Social Club still stands today in the city of Tianjin, China, complete with musty, chandeliered corridors; a grand staircase; a dark wood-paneled billiards room; and a grand ballroom populated with geriatric ballroom dancers. As one meanders its creaky wooden floors, it is easy to imagine how the life and times of the colonial businessperson differed from that of today's, and that communications would be at the top of the list. Colonial businesspeople communicated with the "home office" back in England by Royal Mail Ship perhaps only four or five times per year, whereas modern international businesspeople can be assured that a large number of e-mails from the head office are waiting in their in-boxes every morning.[10] Colonial-era businesspeople were, by necessity, more independent and more self-sufficient than their modern-day counterparts. While it is tempting to wax lyrical about "the good old days," the relationship between head office and in-country operations has always been a key to success or failure. At Hershey, Johnson at the international head office set overall strategy and his subordinate Porter in China was given the freedom to implement it as conditions on the ground permitted. Working together, Johnson and Porter ensured focused and consistent implementation of strategy, which brought commercial sustainability and fiscal discipline to Hershey's China initiative. This collaboration was the foundation of Hershey's success in China.

* * * * *

By Hershey's fourth chocolate season in China (1998–1999), having established Hershey as a credible chocolate competitor without having built a factory, Johnson and Porter succeeded in achieving their mission to build a low-risk, high-reward business model that provided an excellent platform for rolling out the business in China nationally. When Porter's four-year China assignment ended in 1999 (his assignment having been extended one year from his original three-year mandate), he was replaced by a team of two managers. One was Derek Lai, chief representative of Hershey's China Representative Office and national sales director, a Hong Kong citizen who had spent six years building fast-moving consumer goods businesses in China for a distributor and a European candy company. I was the other member of the team, installed as Hershey China's business manager after nearly ten years' experience building consumer-product businesses in Taiwan, Hong Kong, and Mainland China. With both of us reporting directly to Johnson, Derek would lead Hershey China's in-country sales and distribution operation, while my charge was to provide strategic management and lead marketing.

Pairing two new hires who must find their places in the vacuum left by a single top manager was a risky move, since after 5,000 years of rule by autocrats, Chinese people had become accustomed to the clarity and relative stability of singular and unambiguous centralized leadership, and they had developed an abhorrence for social chaos as the result of destructive political factionalism and infighting. The fact that there were suddenly "two bosses" at Hershey China where there used to be only one raised fears that the clear lines of authority would become confused and that political infighting and factionalism might disturb the peaceful and well-ordered social balance that existed under Porter. Had things gone that way, it would have been only a matter of time before the China team either picked sides and joined in the fray or left the company in disgust.[11] Fortunately, Derek and I developed a strong personal friendship, quickly found a balance as co-leaders of the Hershey China organization, and committed ourselves to achieving business success as a unified team. Leading by example, we shared our authority in the spirit of mutual respect, and this was observed by the China team and adopted as the new company culture.

* * * * *

The 1999–2000 chocolate season, Hershey's fifth in China, was marked by an aggressive expansion plan to double geographic distribution to a total of eighteen cities, including cities in the northeast, south, and center of China—just short of a national status but enough to double sales in one season. Up to and including this season, the Hershey's Kisses business grew for the most part unopposed in China's new bite-size chocolate market segment, quickly developing a consumer following in each new city where it was launched. Meanwhile, Cadbury and Mars were slugging it out in a head-to-head battle for dominance of the chocolate bar segment. Rather than cut the retail price and start a price war, Cadbury and Mars entered into a contest of one-upmanship, offering consumer-value promotions. One launched a "10% More Free" enlarged version of its chocolate bars. The other responded with a "15% More Free" version, which was in turn countered by a "20% More Free" version. The contest peaked at "30% More Free" before Cadbury threw in the towel and refocused on the development of its Éclairs business. It was both a painful and a pleasing spectacle for people at Hershey China to watch, and they made the most of their rivals' mutual distraction by driving the Kisses business as hard as they could within their eighteen cities. Eventually, Kisses made enough of an impact that Mars and Cadbury followed suit with their own bite-size products, and it wasn't long before retail shelf space devoted to bite-size products was comparable to that of the bars.

From launch, there were three Kisses pack sizes: a 37-gram (1.3-ounce) single-serve pack, a 146-gram (5.2-ounce) pack for sharing with friends, and a 340-gram (12-ounce) family pack. Chinese consumers were moving beyond buying chocolate mainly for gift giving and were rapidly adopting chocolate into their self-consumption habits—a key milestone in the development of China's chocolate market. Kisses family pack sales, for example, would peak around family holidays such as the Moon Festival and Chinese New Year, not to be given as a gift but to fill the candy trays people offered to houseguests as a snack. Nevertheless, Kisses remained Hershey's only bite-size product. To fully capitalize on its "bite-size discovery" it needed to expand its bite-size product offering to consumers.

Hershey's Nuggets was the company's next entry into the fast-growing bite-size segment, an effort to stay ahead of the competition. Hershey's Nuggets are mini blocks of chocolate that offer consumers a two-bite portion. The main attraction is the bite itself; American consumers received oral gratification reminiscent of the satisfying bite into the regular-size Hershey's Bar they grew up with and loved. China's new consumers, however, had no such nostalgia about chocolate bars. In the fall of 1999, Hershey's Nuggets was launched in a stand-up pouch as a self-consumption offering but struggled in the shadow of Hershey's Kisses. Nuggets' two-bite attribute was not a meaningful point of differentiation for Chinese consumers, and as a result, the product's sales were well below expectations. In more mature chocolate markets such as the United States there is a dizzying array of products; portion sizes; consumption occasions (e.g., Halloween, Valentine's Day, Easter); and even consumption methods, such as the frozen Snickers bar. The Nuggets launch demonstrated the limited degree of category segmentation that Chinese consumers would tolerate at that stage of their demand for chocolate. In time, China's chocolate lovers would expand their horizons, but in 1999 they weren't quite there yet.

If the tactile sensation of biting into a Nugget was not meaningful to the Chinese, the shape of the Nugget, which resembles a chubby gold bullion, would be appealing. Although Chinese gold was traditionally molded in boat-shaped ingots, the gold-brick image held appeal in the China market and could be used to fill a market segment that Hershey had thus far neglected: the gift market. Although the gift section as a percentage of shelf space in retail stores was shrinking relative to the fast-growing self-consumption segment, it still remained a large and high-profit market segment. Like other chocolate manufacturers, Hershey took its design cues from Ferrero Rocher, which, as we have seen, pioneered chocolate gift giving in China, and the little gold-brick Nuggets were presented to consumers in a transparent gift box. Nuggets succeeded in the gift market, reinforcing the need to remain flexible and reactive to consumer expectations.

Product availability and visibility are essential to the success of consumer goods, especially for those, like chocolate, that rely heavily on impulse buying. Though the growth of hypermarkets and high-end supermarkets during the second half of the 1990s was rapidly accelerating, they were still highly limited in number, and this resulted in a high concentration of chocolate sales in such outlets. This concentration not only corralled consumers into a narrow retail battlefield, it also focused the in-store promotion investment of competing chocolate companies. Furthermore, with as much as 40 percent of annual chocolate sales in China at the time occurring during the two months leading up to and including the Chinese New Year, each competitor in the chocolate arena naturally sought to take advantage of both the physical compression of the market into a narrow range of stores and the narrow time window in which most sales occurred. The result was that peak buying season created havoc in the chocolate aisles of China's hypermarkets and high-end supermarkets. Given the proven effectiveness of sample giveaways within reach of the product itself, and the low cost of employing in-store promoters in China, there were often more promoters than consumers in the chocolate aisle of many stores.

Within this free-for-all was an opportunity to break through with merchandising techniques and tools that had proved successful in more developed countries. One such tool was the lane-blocker display. The vast majority of supermarket checkout lanes are closed most of the day and put into use only during peak shopping hours. A lane-blocker is a display rack on wheels that is rolled into idle checkout lanes during off-peak store hours. This simple device turned idle checkout lanes into additional points of purchase. To make the concept absolutely clear to my Chinese colleagues I brought photos from U.S. retail stores, created flow diagrams explaining how it worked, and even took people to stores and made dramatic sweeping motions with my arms to ensure that there was no doubt in anybody's mind about how lane-blockers worked.

But seeing is believing, and we would need to do an in-store test to prove the concept in China. A Hershey sales representative had one placed in a store, and a month later we visited the test store. We were delighted to see the lane-blocker display in a good position next to the checkout counter, nicely merchandised with a smiling merchandiser proudly standing beside it. The store, however, was a small neighborhood supermarket that had only one checkout counter. When asked how a lane-blocker is used in a store with only one checkout counter, the sales representative explained that when the store is open, the display was put next to the checkout counter, and when the store closed for the day, it was put inside the checkout lane. As to why he chose a store with only one checkout counter to conduct the test, he pointed out that hypermarkets and big supermarkets would not accept the test in their stores. In short, the one-checkout store was the only store where he could get permission to conduct the test. Seeing our eagerness for making the test a success, the sales representative did not want to disappoint, so he did the best he could under the circumstances and hoped for the best. This was a good example of how coming to China with an idea that the market is not ready for can become an exercise in frustration, while also highlighting the Chinese cultural characteristics of feeling embarrassed to say no and the inclination to dutifully tell the boss what he or she wants to hear.

The Sixth Season: 2000–2001

By the Hershey Company's sixth season in China, the brand was established with both the trade and consumers to such a degree that it was possible to further accelerate the company's geographic expansion. Hershey China expanded its distribution to thirty cities and had become a national brand. However, the nationwide success exposed a major handicap in its approach to the market: the long supply chain, from Pennsylvania to far-flung Chinese cities, was stretched to the breaking point. This was most apparent in the difficulty of maintaining balanced inventory levels during the peak season and filling out-of-stocks on hot-selling SKUs. All of the logistics of getting product to market required a minimum two-month lead time—a serious competitive disadvantage to Cadbury, Nestlé, and Mars, all of whom manufactured in China. This problem was exacerbated by the seasonality of the Chinese chocolate market. If you ran short of product during the short peak season, you were out of luck.

Hershey could resolve the supply-chain problem by importing Hershey's Kisses and Nuggets in bulk and repacking to-order in China. If a city distributor in, say Xian, needed more of a particular Kisses SKU, it could be packed from bulk inventory held in China and delivered within days, not months. Though its product would continue to be manufactured in the United States, a well-managed repacking operation in China could finally put the candy maker on a level supply-chain playing field with Cadbury, Nestlé, and Mars. Doing so, however, would require Hershey to step up its level of commitment in China.

At the same time, Hershey was clearly pushing the limits of its representative office legal entity, since such offices are intended for the purpose of only initial business development in China, not as a long-term legal entity. China was eager to see Hershey become a fully operational, tax-paying member of China's business community,[12] and Hershey had more than proved that it had a viable business there. Consequently, it was becoming increasingly difficult to justify Hershey China's status as a "test marketing" exercise, both to the Chinese government and to Hershey's head office. The time had come for the Hershey Company to either go to the altar or call off the wedding in China. In 2001, Hershey incorporated its WFOE[13] in China, and the Hershey Company and the People's Republic of China effectively tied the knot.

The Shanghai WaiGaoQiao Free Trade Zone was selected for both the domicile of the WFOE and the location of Hershey's repacking operation, since it was the most advanced free-trade zone in China at the time and was located in Hershey China's heartland city of Shanghai.

With the location settled, the next issue to be sorted out was the operating costs, and it was expected that, at the relatively low volumes, the addition of the WFOE and repacking operation in China would increase overall cost. However, it was discovered that Chinese-made packaging quality was on a par with, and in many cases superior to, packaging made in the United States, and it could be purchased at a fraction of the cost of American-made packaging. This made sense, since China was fast becoming the preeminent supplier of low-cost consumer goods to the world, which required Chinese-made packaging that would pass muster on retail shelves anywhere in the world. Further, when the duty savings from importing lower-value bulk product was combined with China's low-cost packaging material, in-country repacking would actually provide a slight profitability improvement over the finished-goods export business model. Hershey China had a salable capital investment plan.

In the first quarter of 2001, the proposal to incorporate Hershey's WFOE and repacking operation in China was taken before the company's board of directors and was approved. But owing to a companywide head count freeze in place at the time, Hershey China was not allowed to increase its overall head count. Effectively, Hershey China was approved to incorporate the subsidiary, lease the building, and purchase packing equipment but was not authorized to hire people to run the new operation. Yet people were needed to run the repacking operation once the facility was completed, and if the new Hershey China subsidiary wasn't permitted to hire them, the only choice was to hire another company to hire them.

After a brief search, Edward Keller, a full-service 3PL company that had already established its own operations in the Shanghai WaiGaoQiao Free Trade Zone, was identified and hired to manage Hershey's new China warehouse and repacking facility. In addition to logistics and distribution services, the company provided turnkey facilities management services, including simple repacking. Besides complying with the corporate head count freeze, it was found that there were a number of benefits to having a third party operate Hershey's WaiGaoQiao facility. One was that there would be no learning curve for Hershey in running a repacking and warehouse operation in China. Also, Edward Keller's people already had established relationships with the WaiGaoQiao Zone, Shanghai custom office, and other local officials. Another important benefit was their experience in procuring and organizing temporary labor, which had been a regulatory gray area for multinational companies in China and so was better left to experienced third parties to manage. From a business-development standpoint, the biggest advantage was that the

Hershey China team could retain its 100 percent focus on building its business with Chinese consumers without getting distracted by operational problems, as Cadbury did.

In the end, the head count freeze turned out to be a god-send for Hershey China, since it took the task of hiring and training people to run the warehouse and repacking operation off the company's shoulders. The business license was issued in May 2001, and the following four months consisted of a full-court press to complete the facility installations and to get its repacking operation up and running in time for the start of the next chocolate season, in the coming fall.

Under New Management

A series of management changes had dire implications, not only for Hershey in China but for Hershey International as well. In 2001, Johnson, the impetus behind the creation of Hershey China, moved on and was replaced by an American expatriate living and working in Beijing. Within twelve months, he replaced Derek Lai and nearly the entire Hershey China sales and marketing team with people from his previous employer and distributors that had been with Hershey for years were replaced with distributors that his salespeople had worked with in the past. In the spring of 2002, I was rotated back to the United States, by which time Hershey China was a completely new organization.

The new team was entrusted with running the company's new China WFOE. Representative offices are not allowed to conduct commercial transactions, which means that the amount of money they control is nominal (e.g., petty cash for office expenses). But the new WFOE, on the other hand, was a stand-alone business that controlled funds from sales and payments for expenses in the millions of dollars. Needless to say, the stakes for maintaining good corporate governance over Hershey's new WFOE and oversight of the new China team were raised substantially.

The other significant change of management occurred at Hershey International headquarters, with the dismissal of the Hershey International head at the end of 2001. The Hershey International division was then overseen by a series of four managers in as many years, and the decision was made to shut down Hershey International's unpopular South Florida office. In 2004, except for a few handpicked people who returned to the company's home office, Hershey International employees were downsized out of their jobs and the office in Florida was closed. These radical changes at the Hershey International head office meant that, with revolving-door oversight from the head office, the new Hershey China team was in effect on its own.

With the combined changes of management at the Hershey International head office and Hershey China came changes in strategy, discipline, and control that steered Hershey's China operation seriously off course and eventually resulted in a catastrophic collapse of the company's operations during the first quarter of 2004. Details are sketchy, but people who were there to witness it spoke of office doors being chained closed, computers and records being seized, and a workforce reduction from 170 employees to approximately 10. The collapse of Hershey's China organization resulted in a near complete withdrawal of Hershey products from the

China market over the following two-year period. Hershey was effectively out of the chocolate game in China.

Epitaph

Over nine consecutive chocolate seasons in China, Hershey had achieved number-two market share in Shanghai and was rated among the top three in chocolate brand recognition among chocolate consumers in Shanghai, Beijing, and other key cities. Notably, this was accomplished in head-to-head competition with global-savvy competitors Mars, Cadbury, and Nestlé, which had all invested tens of millions of dollars in manufacturing operations and had up to a three-year head start. But starting in the 2004–2005 season, Chinese chocolate consumers would have a difficult time finding their Hershey's Kisses on retail shelves.

While loitering in the chocolate section of a retail store the season Hershey China imploded, I saw a woman shopper pick up a bag of Hershey's Kisses and, in Mandarin, say to herself, "Little Hershey's Kiss, Big Chocolate Taste." Though I was no longer working for Hershey, it was a poignant reminder of what Hershey had once accomplished in China, only to see it all slip away.

Hershey had come all the way from America to China, and with little knowledge or experience, had managed to succeed in one of the most challenging marketplaces in the world by attending to the basics of the business and by maintaining an unrelenting focus on building its brand with Chinese consumers. But in the end, although Chinese consumers warmly welcomed Kisses into their lives, Hershey left them without so much as a note on their pillows.

CHAPTER 5

Nestlé

China's Chocolate War Sideshow

W hen Nestlé opened its first factory in China in 1990, an infant formula and milk powder facility in Shuangcheng, Heilongjiang Province in the far northeast of the country, Nestlé Group CEO Helmut Maucher was so convinced of the importance of this market that he announced the company would have ten factories in the country within ten years. Indeed, eighteen years later it was operating more than twenty factories there. Few food companies have gone into China with a commitment as strong as Nestlé's.

By 2007, with worldwide sales of 107 billion Swiss Francs ($89 billion) and offices and operations in more than eighty countries and five hundred factories worldwide, Nestlé S.A. was the world's largest food and beverage company. It is a leading producer of powdered milk, milk-based infant formulas, and various other milk products (e.g., Carnation); coffee (e.g., Taster's Choice); ice cream (e.g., Dreyer's); prepared dishes (e.g., Stouffer's); cereal (through a joint venture with General Mills, Cheerios); bottled water and beverages (e.g., Perrier); pet foods (e.g., Purina Friskies); and, of course, chocolate (e.g., Nestlé Crunch).[1] Nestlé's international sales make up more than 95 percent of its total sales (less than 5 percent of its sales are made in its home country of Switzerland), and it is the gold standard for multinational food and beverage companies operating in the global marketplace.

Entering the China market after that country's doors opened in 1978 was a critical opportunity for Nestlé to make the right first impression for its hundreds of products with China's hundreds of millions of first-time consumers. Nestlé's leadership was both visionary and pragmatic, setting the standard for operational excellence for multinationals in China, as it has around the world. Nestlé both manufactures and sells products from all of its product categories in China. By virtue of its size and the depth of talent in its international management pool, it is not surprising that Nestlé in China is a success story.

In addition to being one of the world's largest food companies, it is also one of the largest chocolate companies and is the antithesis of Hershey. Though it is the largest chocolate company in the United States, Hershey has historically sold less than 10 percent of its products outside of North America, and it has struggled for decades to develop a viable international business strategy.

Like the other Big Five chocolate companies, Nestlé chocolate first traveled Hong Kong's modern-day silk road into China during the 1980s and early 1990s. When it finally opened its chocolate factory in Tianjin, China, in 1996, it was poised to become not only one of the largest chocolate companies in the global marketplace but also the largest in China. And China was on track to become the largest consumer market in the world.

A Brief History of Nestlé

Heinrich Nestlé was born August 10, 1814, in Frankfurt, Germany. His ancestry could be traced to the late 1400s; its coat of arms bore an image of a mother bird feeding its babies in a bird's nest, which eventually became Nestle's company logo.[2] Nestlé moved to Switzerland in the 1830s, where it was not yet the prosperous mountain enclave known for discreet bankers, precision mechanical watches, and chocolate that it would later become. Indeed, many Swiss villages were quite impoverished by their isolation among the Swiss Alps and Jura mountain ranges, and malnutrition among infants whose mothers could not adequately breast-feed was commonplace. Nestlé, an inventor who served four years as a pharmacist's apprentice, dedicated his pharmaceutical skills and a large part of his life to developing baby food formulas to reduce Switzerland's high infant mortality, which was closely linked to malnutrition. A milk and cereal formula that Nestlé developed in 1867 was an effective substitute for breast milk, and it became a worldwide commercial success, starting in England in 1868. By the early 1870s, he was exporting his Nestlé's Infant Food as far as Australia and Latin America.

During his lifetime, Nestlé had no direct involvement in the development of chocolate, but he helped inspire it. Nestlé was friendly with Daniel Peter, who invented modern milk chocolate in 1875, and it was Nestlé's experiments with milk-dehydrating processes for his infant formulas that was the catalyst for Peter to experiment with combining dehydrated milk and cocoa bean extracts. Nestlé sold the company in 1874 for 1 million Swiss Francs (approximately US$3.8 million in 2007 dollars),[3] retired in 1875, and died fifteen years later.

It was the Anglo-Swiss Condensed Milk Chocolate Company, a fellow Swiss company,[4] however, that most directly impacted Peter's development of milk chocolate: he used its sweetened condensed milk to produce early versions of his milk chocolate. Nevertheless, Peter's chocolate products, manufactured by his own company, Société Générale Suisse de Chocolat, were marketed under the Nestlé brand name and distributed by Nestlé from just after the turn of the twentieth century until 1929, when Nestlé acquired Peter's company. During the early decades of Nestlé's history, chocolate was a significant part of its business.

In the 1930s, Nestlé began introducing new products and making acquisitions that have made it the highly diversified international food and beverage powerhouse it is today. Over time, the company's chocolate business would gradually be eclipsed by its other food and beverage businesses. For example, in the midst of a worldwide glut of coffee beans in 1938, Nestlé began marketing the first instant coffee under the Nescafé brand. In 1947, it purchased the Swiss soup mix, bouillon, and seasonings company Maggi, and over the next fifty-seven years made fourteen additional major acquisitions and formed four major worldwide joint ventures. Today, its milk, nutrition, and ice cream products account for the largest percentage of the company's worldwide sales, approximately 30 percent, followed by coffee and beverages, about a quarter of its business. Chocolate and confectionery, by contrast, accounts for only 10 percent of total company sales. Nevertheless, so huge is Nestlé that 10 percent is enough to make Nestlé one of the world's leading chocolate companies.

Nestlé's Arrival in China

Nestlé's slogan is "Good Food, Good Life," and as its products began trickling, then flowing, into China through Hong Kong during the 1980s, the company helped bring the good life to the Chinese people, who had suffered decades of extreme privation. Nestlé was unique among the Big Five chocolate companies in that not only did its vast range of products satisfy consumers' desires to experiment with exotic foreign indulgences, such as chocolate, but its other offerings helped meet their health and nutrition needs. Nestlé products would find a home in the cupboards and pantries of Chinese consumers and become a part of daily life for millions—from the purified bottled water they drank and the bouillon they used to enhance the flavor of soups, to the milk they gave their children and infant formula they fed their babies.

Donning the halo of credibility that foreign companies and their brands enjoyed in those days, Nestlé's brand image in China developed first and foremost around nutrition, purity, and product safety. With so much to offer consumers, and with competitors such as Kraft Foods, Danone,[5] and Unilever eyeing the China market as well, there was no question that Nestlé needed to make a major long-term investment there; the only question was when.

That Nestlé didn't open its first food plant in China until 1990 is testament to how far the country had to come with its economic transformation, which had begun twelve years earlier. Though some companies had built manufacturing operations there throughout the 1980s, they were predominantly manufacture-for-export operations such as garment and toy factories, or factories that produced industrial products such as glass and steel to meet the urgent needs of a country whose industrial base required rebuilding virtually from the ground up. Packaged foods and beverages for sale in China were a different story, however. Before it could justify manufacturing in-country, Nestlé had to introduce its brands to Chinese consumers, and China's consumer markets had to develop and grow to the size where they created sufficient sales opportunities to justify such an investment.

Nestlé didn't jump in all at once. The Shuangcheng milk factory that opened in 1990 was the beginning of a phased entry strategy for China that would take the better part of a decade to implement. As individual manufacturing operations came on line, Nestlé products that were being exported to China were systematically substituted with products produced in-country. Eventually, almost every Nestlé food product sold in China was manufactured domestically.

* * * * *

When China announced that it was opening its doors in 1978, it was uncharted territory for consumer-product companies, whose primary mission throughout the 1980s was to get consumers acquainted with their goods. To aid in this effort, Nestlé established its first liaison office in China in 1984 to facilitate importation of its products through Hong Kong from the company's operations around the world. Besides building a ready consumer base for its products once its in-country factories came on line, the 1980s also served as Nestlé's test-marketing phase for all varieties of its products, providing much-needed practical consumer research and market information that would guide its planning for later manufacturing investments. It would take a decade of this kind of brand building and research before Nestlé was prepared, and market conditions were right, to build its first factory in China.

Nestlé started with milk-based infant formulas and powdered milk, a priority since such products constituted its largest single product category, had the strongest Nestlé heritage, and had the largest market potential in China. This is because these products met a desperate need in China. Still reeling from the economic disasters of previous decades, the country faced a major public health crisis: malnutrition, especially among the young. Unable to meet the challenge on its own, China welcomed companies such as Nestlé to help it stem the crisis and, with a long tradition in meeting child-nutrition needs, Nestlé obliged.

The Shuangcheng region of Heilongjiang Province, where that first plant was located, was a desolate and underdeveloped frontier region near the Russian border. The factory brought jobs, training, and cash income for the hundreds of local employees who joined the company and a stable economic opportunity for local dairy farmers who met Nestlé's large and consistent demand for raw milk. Dozens of ancillary businesses also sprung up around the factory, from factories that made the cardboard shipping cases to pack the product to private bus services that shuttled workers to and from the factory. All of this economic activity profoundly improved the quality of life for people living there.

Once an agrarian society operating barely above subsistence level, Shuangcheng and the surrounding region was transformed through a dramatic improvement in the region's basic infrastructure, with newly paved roads, extension of the electrical grid, wastewater-processing facilities, and a new tax base with which to build schools and hospitals. On a wider scale, the introduction of Nestlé's milk-dehydrating and -processing technology to the region unlocked its vast potential to improve the health and nutrition of China's citizens nationwide, by providing national distribution for its milk under the Nestlé brand in shelf-stable and affordable products. Sales from the Shuangcheng factory were a milestone for Nestlé in China: From this point forward, Nestlé was no longer just selling *to* China; it was selling products made *in* China.

After milk, coffee and other nondairy beverages were Nestlé's second largest product category and, therefore, next in line to be manufactured by the company in China. Nestlé established its coffee factory at the opposite end of the country from Shuangcheng, in the extreme south in Dongguan, Guangdong Province. It commenced operations in 1992, and it produced Nestlé's worldwide megabrand Nescafé instant coffee. Like milk powder, it was a dehydrated product that was ideal for a developing country like China. First, it did not need special handling (i.e., refrigeration). Second, it could be inexpensively shipped across the country and easily reconstituted with hot water by consumers. Nevertheless, it was still a bold move to build a coffee factory in a country of tea drinkers. But having had a decade to test-market Nescafé in China, and the experience of over half a century of marketing instant coffee in countries around the world, Nestlé saw huge potential for coffee in China—so much so that it was prepared to make the long-term and sustained investment necessary to not only build its Nescafé brand with consumers but even to teach them what coffee was. Next came Nestlé's bouillon and seasonings factory, which opened in 1994, followed, at last, by a chocolate and confectionery facility with the installation of the Tianjin factory in 1996.

In the United States, Nestlé chocolate products, such as Nestlé Crunch, Baby Ruth, Butterfinger, Chunky, and Oh Henry! have become household names. Around the world, however, Nestlé offers an even broader range of chocolate products. Perugina's Baci Chocolate, from Italy, for example, are individually wrapped chocolates, each with its own love note printed inside the wrapper. *Baci* means "kiss" in Italian (no relation to Hershey's Kisses) and is a boxed chocolate that directly competes with Ferrero Rocher. Smarties are M&M-like candy-coated bite-size chocolate pieces that preceded Mars's M&Ms by decades. And Nestlé's Cailler chocolate bars are just one of its many high-indulgence pure chocolate bars that can be found competing with the Cadbury Dairy Milk Chocolate and Mars's Dove bars on retail shelves around the world. Nestlé's worldwide inventory of confectionery products ranges from premium gift-boxed chocolates to a wide selection of everyday chocolates for self-consumption. With such a diverse menu and product line, the company had many options when considering how to enter the China chocolate market. It chose to lead with one of its best-known and successful chocolate brands, KitKat.

Being of English origin, acquired from a British firm in 1988, KitKat, like other chocolate products, first found its way into China through Hong Kong, selling primarily in the up-market air-conditioned stores in the country's first-tier cities. Though the volume of KitKat that flowed into China during the first half of the 1990s was relatively small, it was Nestlé's best-selling chocolate there.

Nestlé's business managers understood that Chinese consumers preferred to eat chocolate in small portions. However, rather than sell solid chocolate in smaller sizes, the obvious solution, they decided to bet that KitKat's 30 percent wafer and 70 percent chocolate composition would satisfy consumer preference for smaller chocolate servings by virtue of the product's lighter chocolate taste. Thus, Nestlé's first confectionery factory in China would be designed to manufacture KitKat, which would be its lead weapon in China's chocolate war.

From the moment Nestlé entered the chocolate fray, it was the odds-on favorite to win the day. Its Nestlé brand image in China of nutrition, purity, quality, and product safety was the envy of its competitors. And none of its chocolate competitors even came close to the sheer size of the company's investment in China, the scale of its operations, the clout that it had with the distribution and retail trades, and even the impact it had on the development of China's consumer-products market. Nestlé was truly in a league of its own. During the first half of the 1990s, when the Big Five chocolate companies entered the country and engaged each other in the battle for China's emerging chocolate consumers, it was difficult to imagine how any of Nestlé's chocolate competitors could muster a viable offense against this Goliath. Its domination of China's wide-open chocolate market seemed inevitable.

The Birth of Nestlé China

Throughout the 1980s and first half of the 1990s, Nestlé's commercial operations in China were under the supervision of Nestlé Hong Kong. Its head office was established in Beijing at the beginning of 1996, and it assumed responsibility for China's commercial operations from Nestlé Hong Kong, which now answered to the Beijing office. The new legal entity, Nestlé (China) Ltd.[6] was the first management company of its kind authorized in China, and its purpose was to coordinate the activities of all of Nestlé's various manufacturing companies throughout the country.[7] By moving its executives to Beijing, the company put them directly in touch with the China market, a cultural immersion that was lacking in Hong Kong's modern high-rise office towers with the occasional visit to mainland China. They would get to know firsthand the very consumers they hoped to seduce whenever they shopped for food at China's burgeoning supermarkets, and they would rub elbows with their hosts at tourist sites, airports, train stations, restaurants, the office, and virtually everywhere else.

However, building a cohesive in-country organization required more than simply getting people together in one place. They needed to be brought together into a unified team, an organization that had a single identity, rather than a collection of people working for various manufacturing companies.

And, building such an organization required strong central leadership.

Bringing its hundreds of products to market in China, and building the factories to produce them, was a monumental task that required both exceptional and stable leadership that Nestlé already had within the ranks. Unlike Hershey, which had only a handful of internationally experienced leaders to draw upon, among Nestlé's quarter-million employees[8] were thousands of career expatriates—a virtual army of experts of all functions—who had successfully established company businesses and operations in dozens of countries worldwide.

While frequent changes of Cadbury's in-country leaders never allowed its unstable organization to gel into a cohesive force, Nestlé China had only three market heads (the title the company gave to the individual ultimately responsible for all that happens within a market, be it an individual country or group of countries) in the more than twenty years between the mid-1980s and 2007.[9] Thus, its leadership in China was both stable and long term.

This stability at the top was matched by the long-term commitments (through long-term assignments) of other members of Nestlé's in-country management team—more than a hundred career expatriates who filled key roles, from factory managers and engineers to business and sales managers. Not only did Nestlé have the name recognition and material resources to dominate the playing field, it had human resources with deep international experience as well.

Of the three men who led Nestlé in China, none had a greater impact than Hans Kruger (not his real name), whose tenure ran from 1998 to 2007. Kruger hailed from the German-speaking part of Switzerland, whose people are known for their diligence and strong work ethic. He began his career with Nestlé as an auditor and eventually enlisted as a lieutenant in Nestlé's expat army when he accepted an assignment in Hong Kong. He later served in the Philippines, Pakistan, and Taiwan, rising through the ranks to become the Nestlé Korea market head before accepting his assignment as the head of Nestlé China.

Tall and lanky, he was an imposing figure, with large hands that he used in extravagant gestures to reinforce his often lengthy verbal discourse with his employees. With a sharp intellect and unyielding determination, he always had a clear vision of what he wanted to accomplish and couldn't comprehend why others might not feel privileged to join him on his obsessive journey toward perfection. Comfortable wielding power and commanding his troops from the head of the massive table located in a boardroom next to his office, and always flanked by his key lieutenants, Kruger was firmly in control of his theater of operations. His boardroom became the nerve center of the organization, its war room, where he and his senior management team plotted strategy and issued commands that were disseminated throughout the organization.

But Hans Kruger was something of a split personality. On the one hand, he cared deeply about people and assumed the role of patriarch to the 10,000-strong Nestlé China family. He would take it as a personal loss, for example, when an employee in good standing with the company decided to leave and would stop whatever he was doing to meet with that person one-on-one in order to try to convince him to stay. And, like leaving the door unlocked for the prodigal son to return, he made it clear that if the employee left the company on good terms and did not work for a direct competitor, he was welcome back anytime. Kruger also cared passionately about the impression that Nestlé made wherever he worked. Having spent the majority of his career and much of his life living outside of his home country, he had developed a sense of personal responsibility in serving as the company's goodwill ambassador and saw Nestlé as a guest that needed to show grace to its hosts.

On the other hand, Kruger's deep emotional involvement with his work and with Nestlé often led to extraordinary demands on and expectations of his employees, with an intensity that was tough for many to take. Most often, his heavy-handed manner was felt by his senior management team. Kruger's modus operandi was to continually challenge the team, often in a blunt and direct fashion, and to such a degree that two categories of people eventually emerged: the favored and the victims. The favored enjoyed the charming side of his personality, and while never a free ride, at least communication was two-way and one's dignity would remain intact at the end of the day. The victims, on the other hand, suffered immensely under the weight of relentless public intimidation and, locked into long-term assignments with some lasting well over half a decade, the boardroom became a chamber of horrors—a recurring nightmare that began when the alarm clock rang each morning.

Kruger's boardroom became a cocoon that enveloped senior staff for countless hours of discussion and debate of even the most mundane minutiae. He expected others to match his level of commitment to the Nestlé China mission. One-day meetings that began on Friday morning would go late into the evening and be carried over to the following day, often even into Sunday—whatever it took. Senior staff could never confirm a dinner appointment Monday through Saturday, since they were on call every moment of the day and evening. The typical workday rarely ended before 9 P.M. To survive, the senior staff developed a gallows humor about their predicament. A day after several North Koreans had jumped the Canadian Embassy wall in Beijing seeking asylum, one of Kruger's senior staff mused in speaking with his colleagues, "If I jumped the wall of the Swiss Embassy, I wonder whether they would give *me* asylum so I can go back home."

Kruger was Nestlé's man in China for nearly a decade and, as enigmatic as he was, he consistently made decisions based on principle and a deep reservoir of knowledge and experience with the company. And, he would define Nestlé's role in China's chocolate market, perhaps for decades to come.

* * * * *

When Kruger took the reins in 1998, China's consumer markets were crossing a major developmental threshold. During the first half of the 1990s, Nestlé and others enjoyed a success borne of curiosity. The novelty of their products created a "market pull." This phenomenon began to fade in the mid- to late 1990s; the novelty of many new products had worn off and demand needed to be driven by other factors. By the late 1990s, the company had invested a great deal of money in China, but most of it was spent building factories to ensure supply. Kruger recognized this and quickly reoriented Nestlé China by focusing its efforts on generating demand for its products through extensive advertising and marketing cam-

paigns, and aggressively driving distribution and in-store promotion of its brands.

At the same time, Kruger understood the risks involved in
making long-term investments in China that might never see
a return, owing to unexpected competitive developments,
changes in government policy, changing consumer dynamics,
or any number of unforeseen reasons. As the market head, it
was his responsibility to protect the company from this kind
of risk. Therefore, in addition to investing in generating demand to accelerate sales growth, Nestlé China also needed
to start delivering more profit in China. Meeting these two
priorities simultaneously had the effect of dramatically shortening its return-on-investment horizon, and consequently the
products that had larger market sizes and nearer-term return-
on-investment prospects would receive priority with the company's investments in demand generation. Given that China's
chocolate market at the time was one of the smallest that Nestlé China competed in, the new company-wide marching
order for profitable growth would have a profound impact on
the company's approach to building its chocolate business in
China.

Sweating the Assets and Reducing KitKat's Cost

When Nestlé opened its Tianjin chocolate and confectionery
factory in 1996, it was equipped with specialized wafer- and
chocolate-making machinery to produce KitKat. Like other
multinational chocolate companies, Nestlé expected the installation of the factory to be accompanied by a dramatic in-

crease in sales. However, as the other companies also learned to their dismay, demand didn't always live up to expectations. The factory's production capacity was not well utilized, and it consistently lost money. Achieving profitable growth with Nestlé's chocolate business would require significant changes to both its product's cost and its approach to generating demand.

When Hershey discovered that its Kisses sold better than Hershey's Bars, it simply reduced orders for the latter and increased orders for the former from its North American plants. Nestlé China didn't have the option of changing to a better-selling or better-margin product, since the investment was already made in the specialized production machinery for producing KitKat. Investing in new equipment to initiate a new product direction was inimical to the immediate goal of achieving profitable growth. So Nestlé needed to find a way to "sweat the assets" of the existing KitKat production machinery by lowering the cost of operation.

In 1999, Nestlé's global research and development labs provided the answer. It had just completed a multiyear research and development effort to produce a sophisticated proprietary compound chocolate (that is, chocolate made with a cocoa butter substitute) that was ready for industrial implementation. Since cocoa butter is the most expensive component of chocolate, using the new formula for KitKat would help achieve profitability by lowering product costs. Indeed, the compound chocolate was so much less expensive that the company could even afford to reduce the price of the chocolate bar. The new chocolate also added some degree of enhanced protection against heat damage, helping to maintain a quality appearance after passing through China's still-underdeveloped chilled supply chain. Without extensive consumer research, Kruger quickly decided to switch Nestlé China's KitKat from its cocoa butter–based chocolate formula to the new compound chocolate.

There were two trade-offs Nestlé needed to make with the formula change, however. First, Chinese labeling laws required that chocolate without cocoa butter be labeled as such. Therefore, wherever KitKat packaging used the word *chocolate*, it needed to be followed by the words *cocoa butter replacer* in parentheses. Second, although it was one of the best compound chocolates to date, it still didn't deliver the same sensation and lingering chocolate taste that the cocoa butter formula chocolate did. Kruger and Nestlé China's business executives were convinced that Chinese consumers' lack of knowledge about chocolate would mitigate the impact of the cocoa butter replacer message, and that the high percentage of wafer in KitKat would largely conceal the compound chocolate's tactile and taste shortcomings.

In addition to reducing manufacturing costs, another area of the business that could provide a substantial cost savings was advertising. During the early days of its launch in China, KitKat received a fair amount of advertising. Since the cost of television advertising in China was on par with that of some of the most expensive cities in the United States, pulling the plug on it would dramatically improve the profitability of Nestlé China's chocolate and confectionery business. Advertising was not banned per se. But having already cut the cost of production, and with plans to pass on a substantial amount of that savings to consumers by way of a price reduction, there needed to be a dramatic increase in KitKat's sales volume in order to generate the revenue required to support advertising while also improving profitability. This was indeed a catch-22: a higher sales volume was needed in order to justify advertising, and advertising was needed to build higher sales volume. In the end, it was a problem that the company's chocolate and confectionery business managers would struggle with for years to come.

Thus, in 1999 Nestlé became the only one of the Big Five chocolate companies to market a compound chocolate in China while abstaining from advertising its chocolate products. KitKat's retail price was reduced and Nestlé implemented a low-price distribution-driven strategy as the way to attract China's emerging chocolate consumers.

The Launch of Nestlé Wafer

In the United Kingdom, Nestlé makes a delicious snack called Blue Riband, a chocolate-coated layered wafer biscuit shaped in a single rectangular bar; it is 70 percent wafer and 30 percent chocolate by weight—the opposite of KitKat. There was a plan to produce a similar product at the company's Tianjin factory, but it was shelved some years earlier. Existing equipment at the factory could be used to produce it with only a nominal purchase of parts. In July 1998, again with no market or consumer research, Kruger decided that the company would immediately move to produce the product, to be renamed, simply, Nestlé Wafer. It was crispy, like a biscuit, rather than smooth and creamy, like chocolate, and to signal this to consumers an image of a shark biting into the wafer adorned the product.

By the late 1990s, the biscuit, crackers, and cookies categories had become fairly well established in China, with an entire aisle or more of shelf space being dedicated to these products in retail stores. Though Nestlé's new chocolate-coated wafer was unique at the time, there was substantial competition from both multinational (e.g., Kraft) and local companies with other biscuit and snack products. Rather than sell the Nestlé Wafer with the competition and split up KitKat and Nestlé Wafer in stores, the company insisted that they both be sold in the chocolate aisle. This not only minimized side-by-side competition with other biscuits and snack foods, but when sold in the higher-priced chocolate section, Nestlé Wafer offered a more visually impressive value proposition, since chocolate was selling at approximately three times the price per gram.[10] It was an extraordinarily short three months from the time Kruger gave the go-ahead to Nestlé Wafer to the date it first rolled off the production line in October 1998—a time frame virtually unheard of in the confectionery industry.

Given KitKat's less than stellar sales track record in China, Nestlé China's confectionery business was increasingly being viewed as somewhat of a problem child by the distribution and retail trade and even some company employees, particularly salespeople. To make the reduced-price KitKat chocolate bar and new Nestlé Wafer a success would require changing some minds about the company's confectionery business in China and about how profitable growth might be achieved. Kruger would lead the charge, using the launch of Nestlé Wafer to demonstrate how it is done, while at the same time dispelling popular myths that had grown up around doing business in China.

For example, Kruger would not accept "the China market is difficult" excuse, a common explanation for KitKat's historic underperformance. Arguing over sales targets being too high or too low was meaningless, he said, since no one knew the true extent of the opportunity that existed in a market of over 1 billion people undergoing rapid economic change. He also refused to accept the widespread belief that China's supply chain was an irretrievable nightmare that severely limited business growth, particularly relevant to the chocolate business given its need for a continuously chilled supply chain. Rather, he believed that although the country's supply-chain systems and methods did not resemble those of developed countries, it could be made to work if people utilized what was available and properly wielded the profit incentive with China's highly entrepreneurial businesspeople.

To show the rest of his troops how it was done, Kruger personally assumed the role of product manager for the Nestlé Wafer, a job that would usually go to someone much more junior in the organization. To achieve his goal of profitable growth, there was to be no advertising to drive demand for the product until its sales volume justified it. Only the power of the Nestlé brand and making the product available, visible, and within reach of the consumer in retail stores would be the key demand drivers. Kruger turned Nestlé Wafer's limited production capacity[11] into an advantage by announcing that distribution during product launch was to be limited to Beijing. He shrewdly used this as part of his pitch to distributors and retailers in order to pique their interest in the new product. The pitch was that the product was brand new, that there was nothing else quite like it on the market, that its retail price was only RMB 1 ($0.15) per bar, that it would have only limited distribution, and that they would be the first ones to have it.

There was one condition, however: the distributors and stores had to pay cash-on-order (COO). Furthermore, supply of the Nestlé Wafer would be contingent upon also paying COO for all the other Nestlé items on the order. The reason for this last condition was that Nestlé had historically offered credit trading terms in China and, like all companies that offered it in those days, had difficulties with collections. Kruger had been working on a wider initiative at the time to move the company to an exclusive COO payment policy and effectively used the launch of the Nestlé Wafer as an example—to help convince both the distribution trade and many within the Nestlé China organization that it could be done. In spite of what appeared to be conflicting priorities and overburdening the launch of the Nestlé Wafer with fulfilling multiple agendas, it worked.

Within a year of launching Nestlé Wafer, the Tianjin confectionery factory became profitable. By its second season, a white version of the Nestlé Wafer was launched, called simply Nestlé Milk Wafer. Sales and distribution of Nestlé Wafer expanded rapidly, first throughout the northern region of China, then nationally, and its Wafer sales quickly surpassed those of KitKat. A concept for a television ad was developed but dropped, since the brand continued to grow without it and the product consistently sold out its maximum production capacity, even through several plant-capacity increases. Having struggled to hit its confectionery sales target for years, the Nestlé China sales team eagerly embraced the Nestlé Wafer. It was the high-growth bright spot in an otherwise stagnant business. Indeed, Nestlé Wafer even boosted KitKat sales, since the Wafer had "coattails," pulling the KitKat along with it through the supply chain until it petered out around 2004, having reached a sales plateau of about 2,000 tons per year. Nestlé Wafer sales, however, continued to grow rapidly every year. By 2006, sales of Nestlé Wafer in China surpassed the 10,000-ton mark. The next year sales hit 14,500 tons.

The secret to Nestlé Wafer's success in China lay in a combination of factors. During its launch, Kruger's "people want most what they can't have" sales approach with the distribution trade worked, and the limited-supply approach served to reinforce the image that Nestlé Wafer was a must-have hot-selling product. He was able to do this largely because it effectively leveraged the power of Nestlé's brand credibility—if it is from Nestlé and hard to get, it has to be good. Also, because Kruger personally championed the product, it became a high priority within Nestlé China, and it energized its vast sales team and distribution network to aggressively build distribution for the product. Further, Nestlé Wafer's affordable price allowed it to reach a much broader base of consumers than a high-priced chocolate would have. Finally, it was simply a tasty and affordable snack that appealed to a large number of consumers and consequently it grew like a weed. Without doubt, in the Nestlé Wafer, Kruger confounded the skeptics and found a way to succeed with the company's confectionery business in China under his own profitable growth mandate.

However, the unqualified success of the Nestlé Wafer and its impact on Nestlé China's confectionery business would be reminiscent of the lessons of the Chinese fable *Shou Zhu Dai Tu*. Translated as "Standing by a tree stump waiting for rabbits," the story concerns a farmer who early one morning, with a straw hat on his head and a hoe over his shoulder, set out along a well-trod path to tend to his fields. On the way he startled a rabbit, which bolted from the path, running head-long into a tree stump, knocking itself unconscious. Delighted at his good fortune, the farmer picked up the rabbit, took it home to his family, and had a wonderful meal. The next day, leaving his hoe behind, the farmer returned to the tree stump where the rabbit had knocked itself out the day before. He sat near there all morning and all afternoon, waiting for another rabbit to come by and make the same fatal mistake, but none came. He waited until sundown, when he gave up and re-turned home empty-handed. The next day the farmer re-turned, again waiting all day with no result. He did this day after day, week after week, and month after month, neglecting his fields, which went untended. Harvest season came and went, but still every day he remained by the stump waiting for another rabbit to come by. And if he had not starved to death, he would still be waiting there today.

Launched in three months, with virtually no investment in product development, plant, and equipment, made mostly of wafer and inexpensive compound chocolate, with no adver-tising spending, sold on COO trading terms and to consumers in two-dozen-piece packages, the success of Nestlé Wafer set extremely high expectations for KitKat and other chocolate products the company would bring to market. Having showed the way with Nestlé Wafer, Kruger expected that the com-pany's other confectionery products be built under a similar business model. Over the years that followed Nestlé would discover whether the Nestlé Wafer business model was re-peatable with its chocolate products or whether, like the farmer, it would wait in vain for another stroke of good fortune.

In the Shadow of Nestlé Wafer

Though Nestlé Wafer initially helped KitKat achieve broader distribution in China, the chocolate bar's sales were unable to exceed 2,000 tons in a chocolate market that was growing at 15 to 20 percent per year. Something was amiss. Though some consumers likely passed on KitKat because it didn't contain cocoa butter, it was not a significant factor in holding back KitKat's sales growth. Its main challenge was that it was too closely associated with the Nestlé Wafer, and its packaging was largely to blame.

Retail stores are a kaleidoscope of colors and shapes. With about 10,000 items in the average American supermarket, it is easy for a single product to be overlooked. One technique for getting consumers' attention and wielding stopping power (that is, stopping consumers from overlooking a product and passing it by as they shop) is unified branding and packaging—that is, multiple products under a single brand with similar packaging. This works well for some products, but it generally doesn't work well for chocolate. And that's a key mistake Nestlé China made with KitKat.

Both Nestlé Wafer and KitKat's packaging designs were very similar. The Nestlé China logo[12] was spread across nearly the entire top half of the product, with the logo lettering in white and the dominant background color red. When KitKat and Nestlé Wafer were sold side by side, they created an eye-catching red block on retail shelves, nicknamed Nestlé's "Great Red Wall." Though the wall was a Nestlé beacon for consumers entering the chocolate aisle in stores, it was difficult to tell a KitKat from a Nestlé Wafer without close examination of the label. Without consumer communication, through either advertising or packaging (the Nestle Wafer's shark image really didn't tell consumers much about the product), Chinese consumers were left to figure out for themselves what the difference was between the two products. The most apparent difference was size and price. Since Nestlé Wafer was almost twice as large and sold for less than half the price, it appeared to be the far better value, and KitKat struggled for its own identity.

Requests to differentiate KitKat from Nestlé Wafer by enhancing its brand on packaging[13] were denied. Kruger was convinced that all company products would sell well under the Nestlé brand and that marketing multiple brands was a far more expensive proposition than marketing multiple products under one brand with unified packaging. There would be no abandoning of this strategy. KitKat, a chocolate bar, therefore took its place in a high-end niche of the chocolate-coated wafer category, and at sales of 2,000 tons per year, this proved to be a sustainable niche in China's confectionery market. But Nestlé would face more significant problems with its compound chocolate, ad-free marketing, and unified packaging approach when it attempted to build a business in the core segment of China's chocolate market: chocolate bars.

* * * * *

In 2000, the Tianjin factory began producing a range of solid molded chocolates using compound chocolate. The products failed to reach a sustainable sales level within two seasons and were withdrawn from the market. It seemed that the company's initial assessment of the compound chocolate was correct: on its own it was unable to deliver a cocoa butter chocolate's smooth feel and rich taste that consumers were expecting from chocolate.

Nestlé China's next chocolate effort was to launch a product similar to Nestlé Crunch, one that contained a high percentage of crisped rice that would mask the compound chocolate's shortcomings. It was launched in 2002 under the same Nestlé master-brand and red unified packaging as the Nestlé Wafer and KitKat—adding another brick to Nestlé's "Great Red Wall." Again, with no media spending, and well hidden within Nestlé's "Great Red Wall," Nestlé China's Crunch sales were dismal. One explanation for this underperformance was that the product was in direct competition with those of the other Big Five chocolate companies, who were all aggressively advertising on television during the chocolate peak season, a key battleground in China's chocolate war, and it was suggested that Nestlé was unable to compete in the chocolate bar segment without advertising. This argument received a cool reception from Kruger. After all, he had launched the Nestlé Wafer without advertising and it was successful. He made it clear that advertising was permissible as long as the business plan included profitability. Nestlé's chocolate and confectionery business would not be allowed to go backward. Confronted once again with the sales volume versus advertising paradox, chocolate and confectionery business managers were unable to build a sales volume with Nestlé China's Crunch that could fund advertising, and it was pulled from the market after the 2005–2006 chocolate season, owing to poor sales.

In a desperate attempt to successfully bring another chocolate product to market in China, Nestlé borrowed an idea from its Swiss market, a novelty item called the Nestlé Cailler Table Bomb. The name was apt. The Table Bomb was a handful of individually wrapped, bite-size chocolates within a mortarlike cardboard cylinder that had a tiny explosive charge at the bottom with a fuse sticking out. It was commonly used at birthday parties, where, at the high point of the celebration, consumers would light the fuse, the charge would explode, and the chocolate would pop out of the top of the cylinder and come cascading down on the table for all to enjoy. In all the excitement, consumers tended to overlook the sulfuric smell that lingered. Still, it seemed like a natural for China, where fireworks were invented and continued to be a big part of Chinese life.

The Table Bomb was slated for China during the 2005–2006 chocolate season, though it would require some modification. It was unlawful to put fireworks together in the same packaging with food products—a sound policy, since fireworks are toxic. Also, each province required individual permits to transport fireworks across provincial borders, and Nestlé would need to acquire twenty-two of them to distribute the product nationwide. The solution was an internal cylinder of compressed air, an idea borrowed from confetti poppers that are frequently used at Chinese weddings and that generate a "pop" powerful enough to send confetti flying across the room. Chocolate is, of course, much heavier than confetti and various pressure levels would need to be tried. Late-night product-testing sessions at Nestlé China's head office resulted in some tests achieving only a halfhearted pop, which blew the lid off the top but left the chocolate still inside the package. Others pushed the chocolate out with such force that it nearly imbedded pieces of chocolate in the ceiling tiles. Through trial and error, the right pressure was achieved, and the product was aptly named the Nestlé Celebration. Though Nestlé fielded tens of thousands of these chocolate mortars in China's chocolate war, once again with no advertising and insufficient funding for doing large-scale, in-store demonstrations, Nestlé Celebration was only a one-season wonder. Nestlé couldn't interest China's consumers even if its chocolate literally exploded out of the packaging.

* * * * *

Before the Nestlé China Crunch was withdrawn from the market, a panel of regular chocolate consumers was asked to work as a team to sort a wide variety of chocolate and confectionery products that were randomly piled on a table. The products included Nestlé Wafer, KitKat, and China Crunch bars, along with products from Mars and Cadbury (Hershey was absent, since it was being withdrawn from the China market at the time), some local chocolates, and an assortment of multinational-brand wafers and biscuits. After several minutes, the Dove, Cadbury, and imported chocolates ended up in one pile, the local chocolates in another, and the wafer and biscuit products in a third. Notably, the consumer panel had pulled all Nestlé products together into one big red pile and then pushed them into the biscuit pile. It seemed that Nestlé Wafer's success, combined with the master branding and unified packaging throughout Nestlé's chocolate range, ensured that all other Nestlé confectionery products—biscuit or not—had been classified as such in consumers' minds.

Though the Nestlé brand was highly regarded, as brand images began to take hold in the minds of China's rapidly maturing consumers, it did not automatically translate into credibility as a chocolate maker. The relentless assault of Dove, Cadbury, and Hershey ads, chockful of luscious images of pouring, rippling, and swirling chocolate, and Dove ads in particular showing consumers enjoying the indulgent pleasure of their chocolate, had established their images as chocolate companies. Furthermore, with all of them selling cocoa butter–formula chocolates, they delivered on chocolate's promise of oral indulgence. If Nestlé really wanted to get into the chocolate game, it needed to rethink its compound-chocolate approach for the China market.

After successive failures with compound chocolates, the company finally launched a range of cocoa butter–formula chocolate bars in the 2006–2007 chocolate season. But much had changed in the eight years since the Nestlé Wafer was launched. China's chocolate consumers and the market had substantially evolved, and generating demand simply by being available, visible, and within reach of consumers was not enough anymore. Consumers needed to be convinced. But the company's cocoa butter chocolates arrived on China's retail scene without advertising to differentiate the product from the competition, and without its own brand or specialized packaging to differentiate them from Nestlé's other confectionery products.[14] China's chocolate consumers were not impressed, and after two years on the market they, too, were on the verge of being withdrawn owing to poor sales performance.

As incomprehensible as it may seem, the world's largest food and beverage company, and the Big Five chocolate company with by far the largest operation in China, found itself unable to bring chocolate to market and sustain it. During the 2003–2004 chocolate season, before some of its products had been pulled for poor performance, senior executives from

Nestlé's Swiss head office went to Shanghai on a personal trip. Nestlé China later received an e-mail from them, complaining about the lack of Nestlé confectionery products in the retail stores they visited. Without the distinctive labeling they were used to seeing on their own products—Nestle Crunch's blue wrapper, the multicolor Smarties label, or KitKat with branding they could recognize to catch their eye—they just assumed Nestlé chocolate wasn't there. Nestlé Wafer, KitKat, and China Crunch *were* there, but they were so well concealed by their unified packaging that they were simply unrecognizable as such. In the end, China's consumers were left asking the same question: Where is Nestlé's chocolate?

Nestlé Could Have Been a Contender

When consumer products began flowing into China during the 1980s and early 1990s, coffee, like chocolate, was a new foreign product to nearly all people in China. National consumption levels were extremely low for both products and virtually nonexistent among nearly all of its predominantly rural population. Consumers were more comfortable giving them as presents, rather than consuming them themselves, and both were introduced to Chinese as expensive and exotic foreign gifts. Since foreign-branded products had automatic credibility with consumers, potential local competitors were relegated to the fringes of the market.

Nescafé first arrived in China in gift boxes that were typically composed of a jar of Nescafé instant coffee accompanied by a jar of CoffeeMate creamer, a pair of cups, and a gold-colored serving spoon. The vast majority of consumers were still in the dark about coffee through the first half of the 1990s, not even knowing how to properly prepare instant coffee. Nevertheless, Nescafé gift boxes were perceived as prestigious and fashionable imported gifts, and were often regiven again and again, since people didn't have much knowledge about or interest in what was inside the jars.[15] Without a large self-consumption consumer base, once the novelty of giving coffee as a gift began to fade in the mid-1990s, the growth of Nestlé's instant coffee business plateaued.

It would be the launch of the Nescafé "1 + 2 sachet pack" in the mid-1990s that would not only get the business growing again but to a large degree establish coffee as a popular beverage in a country of tea drinkers. The Nescafé 1 + 2 sachet simplified the process by mixing a single-serving portion of Nescafé instant coffee, CoffeeMate, and sugar in one package. The Nescafé 1 + 2 sachet taught people how to drink coffee in China, much the same way that the tea bag taught Westerners how to drink tea. Nescafé 1 + 2 sales began to grow exponentially after its launch and national rollout between 1995 and 1997. When Kruger arrived in 1998, he ensured that Nestlé China heavily invested in generating demand for Nescafé through extensive advertising and promotion campaigns. Nescafé has since grown, today being Nestlé China's second-largest revenue producer (behind milk and infant formulas), and it continues to dominate China's coffee market, which is estimated to grow to 300,000 tons, or 230 grams (8.1 ounces) of coffee per person per year by the year 2020.

Nestlé's success with Nescafé, leading the development of an entirely new product category in China, is testament to the business savvy and power of this global food and beverage giant. Indeed, it accomplished the same kind of success with the Nestlé Wafer. However, though it had the power to do so, Nestlé failed to do the same for chocolate. Why did it succeed with coffee where it failed with chocolate?

First, a single serving of Nescafé was far more affordable than a chocolate bar. Value-conscious Chinese consumers could enjoy a cup of Nescafé every day of the week for the same price as a single, indulgent moment with a chocolate bar. Second, coffee's greater affordability offered a much wider consumer base than chocolate's. With the advent of the Nescafé 1 + 2 sachet, it rapidly gained acceptance as an everyday item rather than a seasonal gift or occasional self-indulgent treat. Not only did Nescafé become a household staple for many consumers, but offering visitors a choice of tea or coffee also became a widely accepted practice in offices across China, and Nescafé's add-water-and-stir simplicity fit this need very well.

But perhaps an equally important reason was that instant coffee did not require a chilled distribution channel, which made it far more practical to launch into China's archaic supply chain. A ten-pack tear-off strip of 1 + 2 sachets could be hung from a nail at the window of any one of the country's vast number of mom-and-pop stores and kiosks, and therefore was made available to consumers in millions of points of distribution throughout China, winter and summer. Chocolate's requirement for a chilled distribution channel limited its year-round distribution to air-conditioned stores that numbered only in the thousands.

Coffee, like milk powder and infant formula, was at the top of Nestlé's priority list because it had shorter return-on-investment prospects as a result of its larger market size, and consequently it received higher priority with the company's investments. And not just investments in demand generation, either. Like the milk industry in Shuangcheng, Nestlé had a big impact on the development of Yunnan Province in southern China into a coffee-growing region. Nestlé has spent RMB 50 million (US$340,000) since the early 1990s providing free technical assistance to local coffee farmers, for example, and Yunnan is now a major source of coffee beans for Nestlé China.

Even though Nestlé had the ability to similarly direct the development of China's chocolate market and establish its chocolate as the preferred taste in China, it did not lead this charge since chocolate's smaller and more narrowly focused market (owing to both price and distribution limitations) was unable to provide a near-term return on investment. Nestlé simply had bigger fish to fry in China.

The Last Word on Nestlé, Chocolate, and China

Switzerland is known for producing some of the world's best chocolate, and the Swiss company Nestlé has a vast range of chocolates that could have easily delivered on the indulgent eating experience that was the expectation of China's first generation of chocolate consumers. But these products were never fielded in China's chocolate war. Instead, the company took a low-cost, low-price, and low-investment approach that, with the exception of KitKat, did not meet Chinese consumers' expectations for chocolate, and thus proved unsustainable. Its repeated failures to launch and sustain a chocolate bar, the core of any chocolate market, ultimately had very little impact and was a minor footnote in the development of China's chocolate market. And though its chocolate-coated wafer was a commercial success, it was merely a sideshow in China's chocolate war, establishing a peripheral product that was somewhere between chocolate and biscuit.

Nestlé, however, is a vast and diversified food and beverage company, and this profoundly affected the way it competed for China's chocolate market. Just as Nestlé's other businesses eclipsed its chocolate business during the first half of the last century, the company's larger businesses became a higher priority in China. And given the monumental task of establishing all of its products and operations in the world's most populous nation during the early days of its economic transformation, Nestlé and Hans Kruger can comfortably claim mission accomplished in China. By 2007, the ranking of Nestlé's various businesses in China was as follows: milks and infant nutrition and ice cream, 40 percent; coffee and beverages, 28 percent; culinary, 26 percent; and chocolate and confectionery, 6 percent. This is not too far off the relative sizes of these businesses for Nestlé worldwide and, more important, Nestlé China's confectionery business began delivering year-on-year profit from 1998 onward—something that Mars, Hershey, and Cadbury were unable to do.

By forfeiting the protracted battle for the heartland of China's virgin chocolate market, Nestlé left the chocolate war to the other Big Five chocolate companies. With Ferrero happily occupying its premium imported gift niche, Cadbury mired in its internal issues, and Hershey withdrawn from the battlefield altogether in 2004, it would ultimately be Mars that took the lead, and consequently Mars that would enjoy the spoils of victory in China's chocolate war.

CHAPTER 6

Mars

A Well-Regulated Militia

On a cold winter morning in Beijing during the 2005–2006 chocolate season, at a small-store distributor that sold both Mars and other brands of chocolate, a group of salesmen gathered at the center of a compound of ramshackle, one-story brick and corrugated-metal roof warehouses hidden within a tangle of alleyways behind the city's high-rise office buildings. Their delivery bicycles and tricycle carts were haphazardly strewn about.

The salesmen, who sold the other brands of chocolate, were ill dressed for the weather: no gloves, scarves, or hats. Their clothing was threadbare and dirty. Most had no access to hot showers and hadn't bathed for days. They looked as if they had just rolled out of bed, and indeed many of them clearly had. They milled around the courtyard with their hands in their pockets, smoking cigarettes and stomping the cold from their feet.

A foreign executive from one of the other Big Five chocolate companies arrived and introduced himself to the group. They were accustomed to seeing foreigners on the streets of Beijing, but rarely here, in one of the city's minor distributorships, and after a brief pause in silence, the group shuffled into the main warehouse to hear what this stranger had to say. Inside, among jumbled stacks of cases of chocolate and other products, the executive was prepared to talk with the wary group about the product from which they were scratching a living. Perhaps, thought the executive, teaching them about the product's attributes and selling features would help them improve their sales performance. But before he could begin speaking, one of the older men spoke up and complained that it was very difficult to sell product with cold hands. Emboldened, the others soon followed with a litany of complaints about everything from working hours to pay.

In the meantime, on the other side of the warehouse, a very different scene was unfolding. Here, amid neatly stacked cases of Mars chocolate, the salesmen who sold Mars chocolates were clean-cut young men dressed in chocolate brown jackets (with Mars's Dove brand emblem on the back), matching pants, and gloves and they stood in a straight line patiently waiting their turn to collect the product they would try to sell that day to small shops and kiosks throughout the city. Each carried two steel boxes with Dove labels on the side and hooks to attach them to their bicycles—one on each side for balance.

Once they had filled their boxes and loaded them on their bicycles, they assembled in the courtyard for a final briefing
from their team leader. Then they took off, one by one, like
jets off an aircraft carrier, and disappeared into city traffic.

Though both of these small armies of salesmen worked for
the same distributor, Mars had negotiated for a dedicated
sales team to sell its products, and had shared the cost of uni-
forms, bicycles, and gloves with many of these small-store distributors throughout China's first-tier cities. With aggressive
television advertising, the company's Dove brand chocolate
had become a highly visible and dominant force in China's
chocolate market, and its high sales volume made it practical
for distributors to justify the extra cost of outfitting a separate
cadre of Mars-dedicated salespeople like a well-regulated militia. Given the choice of buying Dove chocolate from one of
the well-outfitted "boy scouts," or another chocolate brand
from a nicotine-stained wretch, it was no wonder Mars's success was building on itself exponentially.

The company's success in fielding such a well-organized
and disciplined sales force to sell its products to small retail
stores was representative of its much larger success in China.
After nearly a decade and a half of aggressive engagement
with its competitors, Mars had won not only a dominant
share but also a preeminent position within the country's
chocolate market with its Dove brand, and in doing so had
achieved a decisive victory in its chocolate war. By 2004,
Mars's Dove chocolate led China's retail chocolate market
with an estimated 39 percent market share, with gift chocolate accounting for over a third of its sales.[1] Its China organization expanded to over 2,000 associates, and Mars's total China
sales doubled between 2003 and 2005,[2] with an astound-

ing 59 percent sales growth in 2005 alone. Nowhere in the world did Mars have higher growth and market share. And although the other Big Five chocolate companies had an equal opportunity in China's emerging chocolate market, none of them was as successful in finding the ingredients for success as Mars was.

A Brief History of the Mars Candy Company

Frank C. Mars was born in Minnesota, in 1883, and learned candy making from his mother. Hand dipping sweets into chocolate was one of the techniques that she taught her son, and it would be a skill that he would later use to build a global candy empire.

The story of the Mars candy company began in Frank Mars's Tacoma, Washington, kitchen, where, in 1911, together with his second wife, Ethel, they started making butter cream candies. As the business grew, they moved the operation out of the kitchen and into the Mars Candy Factory, where they made and delivered their candies to local stores daily.

Mars moved back to Minnesota in 1920, to Minneapolis, where in 1922 he introduced the chocolate confection called the Mar-O-Bar. The Mar-O-Bar sustained the company but remained a small regional product that never really took off. The company's famous Milky Way bar, another product of kitchen craft and an idea that came from chocolate-malted milkshakes, was a far more successful product for the small family candy business. Mars created the product by enrobing

in chocolate a bar of chocolate-malt-flavored nougat and caramel.[3] Launched in 1923, the Milky Way greatly accelerated
the company's growth, and the company's annual sales rose
from under $100,000 to nearly $800,000 (just under $10 mil-
lion in 2007 dollars).[4] The ancestor of the Snickers bar—a
peanut, caramel, and nougat candy bar—was also launched
while the company was in Minneapolis, but without a chocolate coating, and it failed to make a big hit with consumers.

In 1929, Mars moved his operation to Chicago, which, as
the nation's key rail terminus linking east and west, offered
broader distribution opportunities. Joined in the business
that year by his Yale-educated son, Forrest, the renamed Mars
Candies Company in 1930 began enrobing the Snickers bar in
chocolate and turned a failure into a huge success. Mars
claims that Snickers is the biggest selling candy bar in history,
with sales that today exceed $2 billion annually. In 1932, Mars
launched the 3 Musketeers bar, another chocolate-coated
candy bar made of chocolate-flavored nougat, and ten years
later, the blockbuster candy-coated chocolates, M&Ms.[5]

Frank Mars died in 1934, leaving the family candy business to Forrest Mars Sr., who subsequently led the diversifi-
cation of the company with the addition of two new product
lines. In 1935, Mars entered the pet-food business and by the
late 1960s was the largest pet-food company in the world; by
2007, pet food accounted for half of the company's total sales.
And in 1942, the company added main meal products, principally the famed Uncle Ben's rice, which by 2007 accounted
for only about 7 percent of the company's total business.

Insofar as its confectionery business was concerned, Mars
was until the late 1980s not so much a chocolate company as
a candy company. Although all of its bars were chocolate-

coated products, there was less chocolate than the combination of their other ingredients, so none of them was a chocolate bar per se. Mars would, however, find success in the chocolate bar business shortly after its 1986 acquisition of Dovebar ice cream, a premium product consisting of rich ice cream covered in a thick layer of high-quality chocolate. Building on the success of Dovebar, Mars launched Dove brand chocolate in 1991, with Dove Promises—individually wrapped bite-size chocolates that, like Perugina's Baci, contained a message on the inside of the wrapper. Dove chocolate bars soon followed, and some ninety years after its founding in a Tacoma kitchen, Mars was in the chocolate bar business.

* * * * *

Today, Mars is one of the world's largest family-owned businesses, with annual sales of $28 billion. Its highly profitable U.S. candy division generates most of its profits, which have been used to drive Mars's global expansion. Mars stays virtually debt free and is widely known as a highly secretive organization that has a closed-door policy toward outsiders. Company owners and executives rarely grant interviews, and even their photographs are hard to come by. As a privately held company, Mars has no obligation to publish its financial data, and acquiring accurate information about the company is famously difficult. The company is known in the industry as a highly demanding place to work, but employees tend to enjoy higher pay than is industry standard.

The company culture at Mars has been described by some of its employees as controlling and parental, yet strangely egalitarian and off the beaten path compared to that of most companies its size. For example, it has been reported that, at one time, Forrest Mars Sr. insisted that every employee, from high-level executive to mail room clerk, punch a time clock. Individual offices were eliminated in favor of an open office where desks were arranged in bicycle-wheel patterns, with managers located at the hub for easier communication with staff.

Forrest Mars Sr. retired in 1969, and leadership of the company was passed to sons Forrest Jr. and John Mars, and to daughter Jacqueline. Forrest Mars Sr. died in 1999 at the age of ninety-five, leaving the family fortune to his children. The Mars family is now one of the wealthiest in the United States, with each of Forrest Mars Sr.'s children reportedly worth $14 billion.[6]

Mars's International Expansion

Unlike archrival Milton Hershey, who was satisfied with the opportunities that the American market offered, Forrest Mars Sr. had a global vision for the family business. Mars's international ventures began when he moved to England in 1932. With a $50,000 stake from his father (about $750,000 in 2007 dollars) and the foreign rights to manufacture Milky Way, he incorporated Mars Limited in the town of Slough and produced the Milky Way bar, renamed the Mars Bar for the U.K. and European markets. From this humble beginning, Mars has grown into a truly global company. Most of the company's sales are now made outside of the Americas: 50 percent in Europe and the Middle East, and 10 percent in the Asian Pacific and Australia regions. The company claims to have facilities in 150 locations around the world and that its products are sold in more than 180 countries.

Mars's legacy of aggressive instincts for international expansion was evident when Mars became one of the first Western candy companies to enter Eastern European markets after the collapse of the Soviet Union in 1991. That same year, Mars was knocking on the doors of Russia and former Soviet Bloc countries with twenty-three tons of Snickers, Milky Way, Mars, and Raider (Twix) bars and was opening offices in Warsaw, Prague, and Moscow. Mars believed that the first company in after the fall of the Soviet Union would win the hearts, minds, and taste buds of those former Soviet Bloc consumers. The only substantial local competition was from Red October, a Russian chocolate brand that was quickly abandoned by consumers eager for a taste of the good life from the West.

Mars's experience in the global market and its penchant for aggressive international expansion would play an important role in the company's success in China. And it was and remains China, with its vast population of virgin chocolate consumers, that represents one of the most promising future opportunities in the storied history of Mars.

Mars's China Market Entry

Although the sheer size of the potential opportunity in China appealed to the ambitious owners and executives at Mars, they understood that their mission there would be to establish their chocolate brands among hundreds of millions of first-time consumers, and that success would require a long-term commitment. But Mars did not have a formal China-specific strategy because it did not view the market as being fundamentally unique. Rather, its executives saw it much as any other market, but with three unusually pronounced characteristics: highly complex, extremely dynamic, and enormous in geographic scope. China's market complexity required an unusually heavy focus on the establishment and development of its in-country organization and the field execution of its product's distribution, in-store merchandising, and marketing activities. The country's rapid rate of change and infrastructure growth would be the company's main mechanism for sales growth, and it would be harnessed by aggressively pursuing achievable opportunities as they emerged, mainly by following the development of the country's air-conditioned supply chain and retail stores. And though the country's geographic size and antiquated distribution infrastructure were indeed a daunting combination, Mars recognized that achievable opportunities for chocolate sales were going to be clustered, initially, in main coastal cities, and this would make geographic challenges more manageable. With one eye on the other Big Five chocolate competitors, Mars entered the market with a simple business model: Go where the consumer economy is growing and, above all, live up to the company's "The consumer is our boss" motto when meeting the needs and expectations of the country's emerging chocolate consumers.

Mars first established a representative office in Beijing in 1990, the same year Beijing hosted the Asian Games, a major sporting event. Mars had a long history of sponsoring major sporting events, and consistent with the company's sponsorship of the 1984 Olympics, M&Ms was made the official snack food of the 1990 Asian Games. In Beijing, in this first major foray into China, M&Ms was an ideal choice because the candy's "melts in your mouth, not in your hand" attribute made it well suited to survive China's underdeveloped chilled-supply chain. M&Ms quickly proved to be a misstep, however. Because of M&Ms' association with cartoon characters and its colorful candy coating, the Chinese perceived the product as "kids' candy," hardly in keeping with the premium, exotic mystique that had developed around foreign chocolate brands. In contrast to M&Ms' "fun candy" image, the company's newest product, Dove chocolate, promised a more rich and indulgent chocolate-eating experience that consumers had come to expect from foreign chocolate brands. Mars quickly switched its focus to Dove.

This was a fateful decision, since Mars's ascension to leader of China's developing chocolate market was mainly the result of the early success of its Dove brand chocolate, which was attributable to three key factors: striking the right value-for-money balance, consumer communication that resonated well with chocolate consumers, and aggressive extension of the brand's cachet across the breadth of China's chocolate market through extensive product proliferation. And in all three of these areas, Mars excelled relative to its Big Five competitors.

When the Mars factory opened in suburban Beijing in 1993, it began manufacturing Dove chocolate bars in China, using the same recipe as elsewhere in the world. Unlike Nestlé, Mars refused to use compound chocolate in order to lower costs, and therefore the retail price. Mars was determined to deliver in China a product of uncompromised quality. Consequently, a single 47 gram (1.7-ounce) Dove chocolate bar would set the consumer back RMB 6 (US$0.88) for the privilege, an expensive proposition for consumers in China at that time. But the relatively high price delivered more perceived value to the consumer, who expected high-quality, foreign-brand chocolate to be on the expensive side.

Paying a premium was part of the gratification, and Dove chocolate bars, made with rich cocoa butter, didn't disappoint. With premium imported chocolate bars such as Lindt from Switzerland and Ritter Sport from Germany occupying the much smaller top end of the market at twice the price per gram as Dove chocolate, and local compound chocolates at the bottom with pricing as low as one-third the price per gram, Dove sat comfortably between the two, delivering a premium chocolate experience at a price that was affordable to the bulk of China's accessible consumers.[7] With an optimal balance of value for money for China's emerging consumers, Dove chocolate rapidly grew to become market leader by the mid-1990s. Its success to a large degree set the market price for mainstream foreign chocolate brands, and Big Five competitors such as Cadbury and Hershey would use the Dove bar as a benchmark for their own pricing strategies.

From its 1993 launch in China, Dove chocolate's packaging has been predominantly chocolate brown on a premium gold foil background, adorned with an image of rich flowing chocolate and branded in both English and Chinese, but with English dominant to affirm its foreign pedigree. Dove's "Silky smooth taste" advertising platform, used in the Mars home market, fit the bill in China, too. It focused on the main benefit consumers were looking for from chocolate: an emotionally satisfying, indulgent eating experience. Communicated primarily through television ads, this message reached consumers by showing people pleasurably indulging in the sensuality of the product. This proved more effective in linking the brand to the mystique of chocolate than was Hershey's more straightforward informational approach, with its early "Milton Hershey/100 Years" ad and Cadbury's practical appeal of "Every 200 grams of milk chocolate contains a glass and a half of pure milk."

Dove's "Silky smooth taste" message was reinforced with images of flowing, chocolate-brown silk fabric, used in all of Mars's consumer communications, from print and television ads to packaging and point-of-sale materials. Most important, Mars has stayed with "Silky smooth taste" as Dove's core message, both consistently and continuously, since its launch in China. Only Ferrero, though spending far less, matched Mars in consistency and continuity with its advertising. Whether on television or in print, Ferrero continuously advertised Ferrero Rocher, and even ran the same "Ambassador" TV ad consecutively for many years. The others of the Big Five, on the other hand, did not fare as well with their consumer communications. Nestlé cut off KitKat advertising during the second half of the 1990s, Hershey ads disappeared with the company in 2004, and though consistent and continuous, Cadbury's "Glass and a half of pure milk" ads were far less effective.

With a product that delivered on its premium and indulgent image, Mars capitalized on this cachet by rapidly proliferating its Dove brand product range into a wide variety of SKUs, ranging from single bars as large as 150 grams (5.3 ounces), down to a 15-gram (0.5-ounce) bar as a mini snack-size offering. One of Dove's more successful line extensions was a broad range of chocolate gift boxes. Starting with solid chocolates in the mid-1990s, and packaged in decorative tins and clear plastic boxes (similar to Ferrero Rocher), these chocolate gifts sold at a retail price per gram comparable to

Ferrero Rocher's. However, it would be a new range of higher-priced gift boxes that would put Mars in a league of its own in China's gift-box market. In 1988, Mars had purchased Ethel M. brand premium boxed chocolates,[8] an acquisition that helped the company develop a competency for making and marketing premium exotic variants such as truffles, cream-filled chocolates, and nut clusters. And like the acquisition of the Dove brand itself, these new Dove-branded chocolate gift boxes would eventually serve the company well in China.

In the 2003–2004 season, Mars launched an elaborately packaged range of chocolates based on the Ethel M range and priced them even higher than Ferrero Rocher—in some cases, up to 50 percent higher by weight. Though the price far exceeded what a typical Chinese chocolate consumer was willing to spend, there was, and still is, a market for them in China. Today, the Dove brand has by far the widest range of types and prices of chocolate, and therefore the broadest market coverage in China, of any of the other Big Five chocolate companies.

* * * * *

While Dove was, and is, clearly a huge success for Mars in China, two of its flagship products, Snickers and M&Ms, struggled to find a niche. When Snickers was launched in China during the early 1990s, China's first generation of chocolate consumers were still able to tolerate only small portions, unaccustomed as they were to the richness and sweetness of chocolate. Unlike most American consumers, who will eat an entire chocolate bar at one time, Chinese would typically nibble at the bars for a day or two, lingering over the experience.

Snickers was positioned by Mars worldwide as a quick snack that would satisfy hunger and provide an energy boost, and that was the marketing approach taken in China as well. However, the thought of consuming a bar of chocolate, peanuts, nougat, and gooey caramel in big-bite fashion to satisfy hunger was abhorrent to Chinese consumers at the time. Knowing the product was high in sugar, they saw consuming a candy bar to satisfy hunger as unnatural. Furthermore, with Chinese pharmacognosy preaching balance as the way to health, people were concerned about filling the body with so much sugar and viewed it as too extreme. Mars responded by reducing portion sizes, but the first generation of chocolate consumers did not take to Snickers in significant numbers when compared with Dove.

In the late 1990s and early 2000s, an entirely new generation of consumers emerged in China, giving Mars a second chance with Snickers. Teenagers who grew up wearing sneakers, riding skateboards, and playing video games were encouraged, through advertising on billboards at China's basketball courts, ski slopes, and other sports venues, and in TV ads linking teenagers, sports, and Snickers, to adopt the bar into their diets. One of the most memorable ads featured a group of old men playing Chinese checkers on a neighborhood basketball court that was invaded by a bunch of cocky teens in baggy shorts, oversized shirts, and baseball caps. The kids challenged the checker players to a game of basketball; the seniors pulled Snickers bars out of their traditional Chinese overcoats, took big bites, leaped from their bamboo chairs, and won the day with moves that were a combination of Kung Fu movie acrobatics and Michael Jordan–style slam dunks. Snickers was a long haul for Mars in China, and though there was no similar product on the market, it took Mars the better part of a decade of heavy advertising and a substantial investment before Snickers finally began to take off with this new generation.

M&Ms, too, were in for a long, slow climb to success and, like Snickers, did not reach a significant inflection point with sales in China until the turn of the twenty-first century. Under Mars's global positioning of "fun candy," the cartoon characters appealed to the next wave of an even younger generation of consumers: China's "little emperors." Like Snickers, its standard-size package was on the large side, so the company obliged with mini M&Ms in smaller packages. Ads featured the world-famous animated M&Ms characters, which connected well with its target audience.

Both of these products are now market mainstays, and so far they have not had direct competition in China from the likes of Hershey's Reese's NutRageous bars (chocolate-coated peanuts and caramel) or Nestlé's Smarties (candy-coated chocolates). Whereas Nestlé, for example, brought its chocolate bars to market without substantial media support, then pulled them off the market when they did not achieve profitable sales within a couple years, Mars patiently stuck with M&Ms and Snickers, allowing consumers' chocolate-consumption habits time to evolve to the products.

Mars Versus Its Big Five Chocolate Competitors

The company's dedication to Snickers and M&Ms demonstrated its commitment to achieving market leadership in

China, and this commitment was also visible in the way Mars met its Big Five rivals on China's chocolate battlefield. Mars is known to be an aggressive competitor, and this was certainly the case as the company did battle with the other companies for dominance of China's chocolate market. Mars was not only reactive to market and competitive developments, it was also proactive and in some cases outmaneuvered the other Big Five competitors in several key battles, particularly in areas in which the company had not traditionally been known.

In the early 1990s, for instance, Mars reacted to local market conditions by switching its product focus to its then brand-new product range, Dove chocolate, after discovering that it most closely matched the expectations of China's first generation of chocolate consumers. And it was also reactive to the market's unusually large gift-box segment by building its own gift-box business that, as a percentage of company sales, was also unusually large—likely larger for Mars in China than anywhere else in the world. Ironically, Mars, the world's leading chocolate-coated candy bar company, challenged Ferrero, a premium-chocolate gift-box maker, in China with its Dove-brand chocolate gift-box range.

Toward the end of the 1990s, when Hershey's Kisses began to make its impact in the market, starting a bite-size craze, Mars quickly countered by launching its own range of Dove bite-size chocolates: mini 5-gram (0.2-ounce) bars in stand-up pouches. Although this range did little to halt the momentum of Hershey's Kisses, whose unique cute and whimsical shape greatly appealed to consumers, when Hershey's China organization imploded in 2004, and Hershey's Kisses were virtually withdrawn from the market over two consecutive chocolate seasons, Dove's bagged bite-size range was there to fill the gap. Mars also aggressively exploited Cadbury China's early flavor stumble with its China-made Dairy Milk Chocolate bars and fought tenaciously to hold on to its gains in the chocolate bar section of retail shelves, effectively blunting Cadbury's attempted recovery of its chocolate bar business.

The company was also proactive and outmaneuvered its competition when, during the late 1990s, and in anticipation of stiff competition with its global competitor Nestlé and its powerhouse brand Nestlé Crunch, it launched Dove-brand Crispy Delicious Rice (direct translation from Chinese) chocolate bars. Like Nestlé Crunch, it was a milk chocolate with rice bar. Its packaging was predominantly red (similar to Nestlé China's entire chocolate and chocolate-coated wafer range), and it featured bright blue borders not too dissimilar to Nestlé Crunch's blue global packaging design. But Nestlé never brought its international formula and brand Crunch bar to China. Rather, it launched a compound-chocolate version under an unsustainable business model that did not differentiate the product from the rest of its confectionery range through packaging or provide for investment in advertising and promotion, and so was unable to establish the China version. Since the Nestlé bar was eventually withdrawn from the market, Dove's Crispy Delicious Rice chocolate was a defensive wall built for a protracted battle that never came. Winner by Nestlé's default in this niche of the chocolate market, Dove's Crispy Delicious Rice currently stands unopposed and, having been proliferated from bars into bagged bite-size and decorative gift-tin offerings, has become a solid stand-alone product range for Mars in China.

Mars met each of the other Big Five chocolate companies

in virtually every major engagement in China's chocolate war, and its commitment to total victory went well beyond the products it launched. The company's will to win was evident in its aggressiveness, consistency, and excellence in execution of other important aspects of its business as well. It consistently outspent its competition in advertising and in-store promotional spending, year after year. Its products were always the best merchandised on retail shelves, offering consumers the broadest possible range of products with the fewest out-of-stocks. It had the largest seasonal off-shelf displays, located in stores' highest traffic areas. And its product was consistently fresher, since the company retrieved substantial amounts of product after each chocolate season to ensure that heat-damaged or expired products never reached the consumers.[9] It was costly, but the company never wavered from its commitment to put the consumer first and act the market leader.

Mars's Commitment to Market Leadership

Underlying the successful competitive strategies and well-executed tactics that Mars employed in winning the hearts, minds, and taste buds of China's first generation of chocolate consumers was its commitment to market leadership. Like Nestlé, Mars in China enjoyed the advantages of a diversified business, with both its chocolate and its pet-food businesses, to spread costs and achieve economic synergies (e.g., there was the opportunity during the chocolate low season to employ idle chocolate-factory workers in the pet-food factory). However, Nestlé's chocolate and confectionery business was only 10 percent of its worldwide sales, and only about 6 percent of its business in China. The other 94 percent of sales were accounted for by much larger businesses such as infant formula, Nescafé coffee, and ice cream. For Mars, however, its confectionery business accounted for over 40 percent of total company sales. Therefore, Nestlé could succeed as a company in China without a successful confectionery business, but for Mars, it was imperative that it succeed with its chocolate business since it was the primary mission there.

Although Hershey was, first and foremost, a chocolate company, it was always ambivalent about internationalizing its business and had only modest ambitions for China from the start. Indeed, its near total retreat in 2004 demonstrated that even having a market presence in China was not a priority. By contrast, Cadbury did have market leadership in mind when it came to China in the mid-1990s, and it showed substantial resolve with its attempts to establish its Dairy Milk Chocolate business with Chinese consumers. But the company eventually fell far short because it could not muster consistent and sustained leadership of the company's China operations.

The extent of Mars's commitment to China was demonstrated in many ways, but especially in its devotion to consumers. Mars recognized that it knew less about the emerging Chinese consumer class than it did about consumers elsewhere. Rather than make assumptions, Mars set out to learn. Company executives spent a great deal of time on the road, walking the streets and chocolate aisles of China's retail stores. This put them in touch not only with consumers but also with the people who knew the market best: the salesmen and retailers. This allowed Mars to drive business growth by expanding the occasions that consumers could embrace its chocolate and experience it.

The company's exclusive in-aisle pic'n'mix[10] islands are a prime example of how Mars's hard-won understanding of consumers allowed it to capitalize on peak-season selling opportunities. Chinese consumers were accustomed to shopping in wet markets and buying from bulk bins, and modern retailers adopted this traditional merchandising technique by establishing a pic'n'mix section in their stores. Though the other Big Five capitalized on this technique, too, Mars was the only company that designed and installed its own stand-alone Dove, M&Ms, and Snickers pic'n'mix displays adjacent to or in chocolate aisles, starting in the 2003–2004 season. Adding these pic'n'mix displays to its repertoire of seasonal off-shelf displays, Mars built a substantial bulk business by giving consumers what they wanted, the way they wanted it, in line with their cultural traditions.

Mars also proved to be a savvy employer in China. When it set out on its journey to build its China organization in the early 1990s, Mars, like the other Big Five chocolate companies, faced the severe shortage of experienced and appropriately educated people in China at the time, and it understood that few Chinese had any relevant business experience that would be of immediate value. Globally, the company built its organization through a formalized company practice it termed "selective recruitment," which focused on selecting prospective employees based on personal traits such as overall attitude, work ethic, and a personal value system that closely match Mars's business principles and culture.

When identifying promising future leaders, the company began by recruiting at the university level, then putting applicants through various psychological-profiling and leadership-style tests to select potential candidates for further leadership training and development. Like Hershey's unconventional "tell me about this shelf" in-store interviews that flushed out the self-confident, commercially savvy, and eager-to-learn candidates, Mars's selective recruitment well fit its massive hiring needs in China by identifying those candidates who had the innate traits and personal characteristics on which the company could build a strong and cohesive organization through training and development.

The company knew that it would be training most employees from scratch, and that training and development would be not only an immediate need but also a continuous process, as people were steadily added to the organization. Raw recruits were put through extensive training and regularly attended sales conferences, as well. Because Mars knew that Chinese prized higher education, in 2003 the Mars Academy was founded to significantly upgrade the knowledge and skills of high-potential company employees, and a year later the Mars China Graduate Development Program was begun. Both of these initiatives not only improved the knowledge and skill of Mars China employees but also established a career path, which encouraged the employees to stay with the company for the long term. The result was an in-country organization with an esprit de corps that was evident, for example, in the company's well-regulated militia of small-store bicycle salesman.

Having successfully dominated the retail shelf space and chocolate sales in China's modern-trade retail outlets (hypermarkets, high-end supermarket chains, and convenience stores), to accelerate its growth and extend its lead, Mars needed to reach well beyond the big retailers in first- and second-tier cities and to drive distribution deeper into the country's vastly more numerous small stores, mom-and-pops, and kiosks (seasonal distribution opportunities as they were). For this, the company developed its bicycle sales force—some employed by Mars and some by distributors, but all focused on exclusively selling Mars products. Whether they worked directly for Mars or for one of its distributors, these cycling salesmen were, in effect, brought into the company by including them in company training and development, as well as in frequently held sales conferences, making them part of a unified team with a common purpose, whose members adopted the Mars mission no matter who cut their paycheck. By 2005, Mars, together with its distributor sales organizations, was making direct deliveries to approximately 250,000 points of sale across China.

The cumulative effect of a decade and a half of investment in and commitment to its people resulted in the emergence of a cadre of Chinese employees up to the challenge of key leadership roles in the company. By 2006, Mars had fewer than ten expatriate managers in China, with the remaining 2,000 or so employees entirely local Chinese. Indeed, the company made good use of skills that were innate to the Chinese people, and part of its culture, most notably the organization and mobilization of large numbers of people. This was highly beneficial to the company, whether it was executing nationwide training en masse or fielding its bicycle sales teams.

Mars's openness to using what was available in China kept its operations manageable throughout a decade and a half of tremendous growth and change, for both the country and the company. For example, rather than try to manage sales and distribution itself during start-up, the way Cadbury did, it engaged a national master distributor. With a master distributor managing the complexities of distribution and collection, Mars was able to concentrate on establishing its brands with consumers, getting its manufacturing operation up and running, and building and training its own organization. It wasn't until the very end of the 1990s, when market conditions and Mars's own capabilities were up to the job, that sales and distribution were brought in-house.

As a privately held company, Mars had a substantial advantage over Cadbury, Hershey, and Nestlé, all of which are publicly listed companies. Though public companies generally have advantages over private companies, such as a greater ability to raise capital, in the case of Mars and China, the publics were at two distinct disadvantages when it came to ownership structure: continuity of leadership and the will to support long-term financial commitments.

With the three children of Forrest Mars Sr. at the helm of the company since his retirement in 1969,[11] the company has had continuity of leadership for nearly forty years. Thus, the same people who established the vision and agreed to the long-term business plan for achieving market leadership in China also saw it through to fruition. With the average Fortune 500 CEO now holding his or her job for just over six years,[12] it is inherently more difficult for public corporations to provide the continuity of leadership needed to sustain a long-term challenge such as building China's chocolate market. In this respect, Mars was like Ferrero, the other family-owned business of the Big Five, which stayed its course for the past quarter-century, though with its more limited vision for a profitable export business to China.

And Mars was at no disadvantage when it came to funding

its China operations. This is because, besides being owned by one of America's wealthiest families, the company has, for the most part, self-funded its way to becoming one of the world's largest confectionery companies (and the largest pet-food company), avoiding the pressure for short-term returns of highly leveraged companies. Mars China became profitable in 2005—twelve years after it opened its Beijing chocolate factory; few publicly owned corporations would have been so patient, waiting for a market to become profitable. To the contrary, the managers of public companies are under great pressure to produce short-term returns to satisfy shareholders, a pressure that often compromises long-term strategic decision making. A good example of how this played out in China's chocolate war was Nestlé's decision to squeeze profitability out of its Tianjin China confectionery factory within three years of its opening. The demand for short-term profitability was a catalyst for its ultimate failure to build a chocolate business in China (aside from KitKat), since the resulting "investment versus sales growth" paradox crippled the company's ability to make the long-term investment necessary to be competitive in the mainstream chocolate market. No, in tolerating the company's many years of consecutive losses in China, the Mars family's commitment to the market over the past decade and a half left a legacy of market dominance in the soon-to-be largest consumer market in the world. And if this legacy for the family's next generation was the ultimate motivation behind their China mission, then winning the chocolate war meant much more to the Mars family than a quick return on investment.

* * * * *

It was, of course, ironic that the Dove chocolate bar, a new product, was the first to have a major impact and establish one of the earliest impressions of self-consumption chocolate in China. However, in a virgin chocolate market, consumers saw little importance in the length of a product's pedigree. Indeed, Ferrero did the same for China's gift-chocolate market in the 1980s, with its then-new Ferrero Rocher chocolate gift boxes.

Emerging Chinese consumers wanted to indulge in this foreign and exotic culinary curiosity called chocolate, and Mars was the most effective of the Big Five in making it available to them and meeting their expectations. In consistently doing so over the past fifteen years, Mars succeeded in its mission to dominate China's chocolate market. Furthermore, when Cadbury tried to match Dove chocolate's taste and tactile characteristics, when relaunching its Dairy Milk Chocolate bars with its new formula in 2002, it was not only imitation as a form of flattery but, in effect, an acknowledgment that Mars had succeeded in establishing Dove as the preferred chocolate taste in China.

Mars won China's chocolate war because of its unwavering commitment to consumers and its determination to become market leader; it was a victory both well earned and well deserved. Mars will no doubt reap the benefits of its early market leadership in the decades to come as the remaining billion Chinese, who have thus far been beyond reach, progressively become accessible chocolate consumers.

CHAPTER 7

Going the Distance

China's 10K Chocolate Race

In 2008, China celebrated the thirtieth anniversary of the country's reopening its doors to the outside world, and it has been nearly a quarter century since Ferrero Rocher chocolate gift boxes were first hand carried into the country as gifts. Since Deng Xiaoping began picking up the pieces of the country's broken economy in 1978, China has transformed itself from an isolated economic basket case to an indispensable economic powerhouse within the global economy. Its GDP has grown by over sixty-nine times, an astonishing 10 percent per year on average, and, having surpassed Germany in 2008, is now the third largest economy in the world, behind the United States and Japan.[1] This historic transformation has made hundreds of millions of Chinese consumers accessible to the Big Five, who challenged each other for their affections and ultimately for the dominance of China's chocolate market. But the Big Five also challenged themselves to find their own formula for success in China's enigmatic marketplace.

In this battle for the hearts, minds, and taste buds of China's chocolate consumers, two products—Ferrero's Ferrero Rocher chocolate gift boxes and Mars's Dove chocolates—made the earliest and most significant first impressions. And both succeeded in large part by delivering on the promise of an exotic foreign indulgence. By being the firsts—Ferrero Rocher as the first chocolate product to enter China, and Mars as the first of the Big Five companies to begin manufacturing chocolate there in 1993—they won the affections of consumers early in the chocolate war, enabling them to achieve their objectives: Ferrero to establish a profitable export business, and Mars to establish Dove chocolate as the preferred chocolate taste with China's first generation of chocolate consumers.

The other members of the Big Five, however, have not fared as well, since in one way or another, they left China's eager consumers wanting. Hershey broke their *hearts* by withholding its Kisses, so adored by Chinese consumers, after the 2004 collapse of its in-country organization. Nestlé confounded their *minds* by switching to less than its very best chocolate in 1998—something consumers expected from local companies, but not from a well-regarded multinational company. And Cadbury offended their *taste buds* by first weaning them on the luscious taste of their imported Australian-made Dairy Milk Chocolate, then inadvertently replacing it with a cheesy-tasting China-made chocolate in 1995.

Though Mars has emerged as the leading chocolate company in China, the Big Five have barely scratched the surface of the country's chocolate sales potential. Indeed, chocolate remains readily accessible to only 300 million of China's 1.3 billion people. Given their extremely shallow market penetration, the past quarter century has been only the initial salvo in the opening battle of the ongoing chocolate war. If penetration of the China market were a 10K foot race, the Big Five might be viewed as having run only about 1 kilometer of it so far. And given the unpredictable nature of China's rapid economic transformation, and the continuing emergence of millions of people into its consumer class each year, the outcome for the remaining 9 kilometers of the chocolate race is still far from certain.

The State of the Chocolate Market: 2008

By 2008, the country's annual growth rate of retail chocolate sales had slowed from approximately 15 to 20 percent to between 10 and 15 percent, albeit on a much larger base than in the past. Though annual retail chocolate sales in China are now approaching $1 billion, it is still a relatively small market, accounting for less than 2 percent of the world's total chocolate sales.[2]

The year 2008 was a historic one for China, filled with both triumph and tragedy. The enormously successful Sum-

mer Olympic Games was preceded three months earlier by
the Sichuan earthquake that killed an estimated 70,000 people.[3] In addition, the global financial crisis hit China hard,
with its GDP growth dipping to 9 percent—only the second
year of the past six that the country saw its GDP growth at a
single-digit level and the lowest since 2001.[4] And the year was
a momentous one in China's continuing chocolate war as
well.

In spite of 2008's economic challenges, it was another
good year for Ferrero in China, with sales growth of its Ferrero Rocher gift boxes slightly outpacing the overall growth
of the chocolate market. The appeal of the imported Italian-
made, gold-colored spherical delicacies has not abated. As of
the 2008–2009 chocolate season, Ferrero Rocher gift boxes
are still being stacked high in China's retail stores, and the
company continues to invest heavily in advertising and in-
store promotions in the run-up to the peak gift-giving season
of the Chinese New Year. The development of a substantial
self-consumption market for Ferrero Rocher, however, remains elusive, though not for lack of trying. One can find its
three- and five-piece self-consumption products being impulse merchandised throughout most modern-trade outlets in
the country's first-tier cities, such as Shanghai, Beijing, and
Guangzhou, but for the vast majority of Chinese consumers
Ferrero Rocher still remains primarily a gift.

Jinsha, the Ferrero Rocher knockoff and local nemesis, is
still on the market, but its presence has dwindled in first-tier
cities as marketing and distribution costs there continue to
rise and where its lower price holds less appeal with these
cities' more affluent consumers. It continues to holds its own,

though, in second-tier cities where its substantial price differential has more impact with consumers.

While it continues to enlarge its in-country organization through additional recruitment of marketing and sales support people, Ferrero still distributes its products through a national master distributor, and the company has not given any indication that it plans to manufacture its products in China. The company's leadership appears intent on staying its course to building a profitable export business there, a business model that has been successful for the company in the past.

* * * * *

In September 2008, the Chinese government reported that over 50,000 people had been sickened, nearly 13,000 had been hospitalized, and four infants had died from drinking milk and milk-based infant formula contaminated with the industrial chemical melamine,[5] and that a host of products from cookies to milk chocolate were contaminated during production with melamine-laced milk. On September 29, 2008, Cadbury announced that it was recalling its China-made Dairy Milk Chocolate because it had tested positive for trace amounts of melamine. Its announcement explained that the tests "cast doubt on the integrity of a range of our products manufactured in China." It appeared that Cadbury's stubborn adherence to its locally sourced fresh-milk production process had found one more way to come back and bite the company. Within days of the announcement, Cadbury Dairy Milk Chocolate was withdrawn from China's retail shelves.

Throughout October and well into November, Mars aggressively filled Cadbury's empty space on retail shelves with Dove chocolates, Snickers, and M&Ms. But toward the end of November, imported Cadbury chocolates began appearing on off-shelf displays and retail shelves in chocolate aisles. And by mid-December, China-made Cadbury Dairy Milk Chocolate (with production dates after September 2008) began to reappear in stores bearing a new yellow ribbon sticker on the wrapper, announcing *nai yuan bao zheng an xin shi yong*, translated as "Milk source guaranteed, enjoy without any worries." To the company's credit, this was a remarkably rapid and well-coordinated rebound from such a widely publicized disaster that virtually singled Cadbury out in the chocolate category; none of the other Big Five withdrew their products in China owing to fears of melamine contamination. The company's resolution of its Cadbury Dairy Milk Chocolate taste crisis during the second half of the 1990s—the cheesy taste of its early China-made chocolate that was the result of substandard milk quality—demonstrated that it had the technical wherewithal to manage product fixes when needed, and those same skills served the company well through its melamine crisis. Only time will tell whether Cadbury's chocolate business will recover from the melamine crisis of 2008.

* * * * *

Hershey is back in China's chocolate war after its unceremonious near-total withdrawal from the market in early 2004.[6] In May 2007, Hershey invested $39 million in a joint venture with Lotte Confectionery Company, a Korean *chaebol* (conglomerate), to jointly manufacture chocolate at a shared facility in Jinshan (near Shanghai) to serve the Chinese, Korean, Japanese, and Southeast Asian markets. China-made Hershey's Bars, Kisses, and Nuggets, and Hershey's Special Dark chocolate have since made an impressive appearance in the country's modern retail stores in first-tier cities during the 2008–2009 chocolate season. But this may be a case of history repeating itself for Hershey—building production capacity before acquiring the consumer base to support it. The company has been down this road before, in Europe during the 1980s, making manufacturing investments under its so-called Patchwork Quilt Strategy. Whether China will somehow be different will be revealed in the coming years.

Though Hershey's renewed efforts in China are impressive, its timing is far from opportune. China's chocolate consumers and the market have evolved substantially since Hershey stumbled on its bite-size discovery with Hershey's Kisses, which it exploited so effectively in the late 1990s; bite-size products are now a relatively well-established segment of China's chocolate market, and Kisses won't have the same revolutionary impact with consumers as they once had. Many regular chocolate consumers in first-tier cities have since established their taste preferences, in large part for Dove, so enticing these consumers to switch brands will be difficult. In addition, the variety of chocolate products being offered to consumers has expanded dramatically, from the addition of Dove's filled chocolates to a plethora of imported chocolates from the world's smaller chocolate players intent on acquiring their share of China's fast-growing chocolate market. Hershey's relatively narrow product range means it will now have to struggle for visibility on a far more cluttered and diverse chocolate retail shelf.

Though exporting from its new China factory to markets in the Asian Pacific region may have been a strategically sound hedge against the risk of possible slow going in China, Hershey's timing couldn't have been worse. The melamine crisis has made consumers within the region wary of all food products coming from China, not just chocolate.[7] Although Hershey does not use Chinese milk in its chocolate (the company claims to have *never* purchased any Chinese milk), the company will be fighting an uphill battle to sell products from its new Jinshan facility outside of China.

But the biggest risk to Hershey's new China initiative will likely be the same as it has always been: the company's historic inability to sustain an investment in an international market to fruition.[8] Though Hershey has showed renewed energy for international ventures in the past two years, with its Lotte China joint venture and another 2007 joint venture in India with Godrej Beverages and Foods, the ensuing global economic crisis will test Hershey's commitment to foreign ventures more than ever. The fact that nearly 90 percent of the company's business still rides on struggling American consumers[9] means the company will be under immense pressure to pull back on long-term investments—especially in international markets—and to circle the wagons around its core U.S. domestic business.

Before its 2004 collapse, Hershey China commanded the number-two market share in the city of Shanghai and was an up-and-coming brand in the more than thirty other cities where its products were distributed. It accomplished this through a relentless focus on building its brands with consumers, while importing its products with only a repacking warehouse and fewer than two hundred people. If the first battle in China's chocolate war over the past quarter century has taught any lesson, it is that success hasn't been about the size of a company's manufacturing investment, but the size of its commitment to the market and its consumers. With its new in-country manufacturing facility, Hershey's vision for the future is to become the number-two chocolate company in China, with a 23 percent market share, by 2010. A very ambitious plan, indeed. It remains to be seen whether, like Milton Hershey himself—who during the first half of his life tried and failed with three candy businesses only to eventually succeed with his chocolate business—the Hershey Chocolate Company will ultimately succeed through trial and error in China.

* * * * *

With the 2007 retirement of market head Hans Kruger, Nestlé China came under new management in 2008, but there have been no breakthroughs or major changes in direction for the company's chocolate and confectionery business. KitKat, which had lost its individuality within the shadow of the Nestlé Wafer, owing in part to its look-alike packaging, was finally brought in line with global guidelines; the KitKat brand on the product label is now much more prominent than the Nestlé brand. However, the brand is still struggling with China's core chocolate consumers and trying to exceed its 2,000-ton annual sales ceiling.

After a spectacular ten-year run, Nestlé Wafer sales have finally leveled off, in part owing to the 2008 general economic slowdown, but also because of increased direct competition from the likes of Kraft Foods Inc., which, in 2006, launched a new variation of its iconic Oreo cookie in China, the Oreo Chocolate Wafer. Designed specifically for the China market, the Oreo Wafer is similar to the Nestlé Wafer, but it adds a layer of vanilla cream in the center to remain true to its namesake. Though it costs considerably more than Nestlé's Wafer, it has largely stopped the unbridled growth of Nestlé Wafer in its tracks. The company is responding with a new television ad, but it remains to be seen how effective it will be in restarting the product's sales growth.

While the 2008–2009 chocolate season was an eventful year for the industry in China, it was another season of Nestlé inaction within the core of China's chocolate market: full cocoa butter bars, bagged bite-size, and gifts. With its Nestlé Wafer and KitKat business having hit a sales ceiling, and its cocoa butter chocolate bars barely able to maintain a presence on retail shelves, its chocolate business is like a stalled car sitting on the shoulder of an expressway as its competitors whiz by, and none faster than Mars.

* * * * *

By contrast, 2008 was a very active year for Mars in China. In addition to expanding its chocolate production lines at its Beijing factory to meet growing demand, Mars began producing chocolate at its new factory in Jiaxing, China, in February 2008. Mars's goal for its Jiaxing factory is to eventually support annual sales of about RMB 1.6 billion (US$230 million), through a production volume output of 50,000 tons.[10] With the addition of this facility, the company is well positioned to supply its rapid sales growth.

Mars significantly advanced its Snickers business in China

with its sponsorship of the 2008 Beijing Olympics. Deemed the official chocolate of the Beijing Olympics, and exclusive candy bar supplier to the food kiosks at events, the company's aggressive media and marketing initiatives surrounding the games helped increase Snickers sales by 75 percent. In addition to increasing sales, the initiative significantly raised the product's visibility and image with its target audience, teenage boys, which is expected to pay long-term dividends for the company.

But by far the biggest news for Mars in 2008 was the company's $23 billion acquisition of Wm. Wrigley Jr. Company. Adding Wrigley's $5.4 billion (2007 worldwide figure) gum and sugar confectionery business to Mars's chocolate and candy business has resulted in the formation of the world's leading retail confectionery company. In China, Wrigley's chewing gum is widely accepted as the multinational product standard-bearer for distribution excellence. Free of need for an air-conditioned supply chain Wrigley's iconic green Doublemint five-stick pack of chewing gum has been made available to consumers throughout the country, including many of the billion consumers who have thus far been beyond the reach of the Big Five chocolate companies. It can be found in virtually every store, large or small, and at newsstands in every train and bus station throughout China. Attendants splay out individual sticks in a fan shape in "complimentary" trays in the bathrooms of China's nightclubs, and restaurants give sticks to patrons at the end of meals as a breath freshener. Like chocolate, chewing gum enjoyed an early success born of curiosity as something foreign and different for Chinese aspiring to the trappings of Western lifestyles. Unlike chocolate, its RMB 1 ($0.15) for five sticks of gum meant it was far more affordable to the masses. If penetration of China's chewing gum market were a 10K race, Wrigley has run about 9 kilometers.

The acquisition promises to have important competitive implications for Mars's chocolate business in China because Wrigley has an unrivaled distribution and sales network there that, at least in theory, creates synergies that will help Mars further advance its chocolate business. As impressive as this merger is, though, it has not changed the laws of physics. Chocolate still melts at moderate temperatures, and chocolate remains a foreign and expensive product for the vast majority of Chinese consumers. Therefore, it is unlikely that consumers will see a Dove bar next to a pack of Doublemint gum year-round in a million kiosks throughout China overnight. But Wrigley's extensive distribution and sales operation gives Mars the opportunity to broaden Dove's distribution to the vast number of non-air-conditioned retail stores each year, as the weather permits. Furthermore, Wrigley's extensive sales and distribution capabilities in second- and even third-tier cities will help Mars get its chocolate in front of more first-time consumers as they emerge there. Other benefits will likely come in less visible ways, such as better margins from shared sales, general and administration expenses, shared distribution costs, and increased negotiating leverage for dominating China's precious and expensive retail checkout displays.

The merging of the two most committed and successful foreign confectionery companies operating in China has the potential to be a watershed event in the ongoing chocolate war. Indeed, it now appears that the other foreign chocolate companies can only hope to coexist with this confectionery empire and maintain a sustainable and profitable chocolate business in the future. Some executives within the chocolate industry are now forecasting an industry shakeout, with consolidation around Mars and the more committed Big Five players, as well as determined exporters to China. But acquisitions don't always deliver as promised or expected, and making accurate predictions about China's rapidly changing consumer market has historically been difficult. It would therefore be premature to begin writing the epitaph of Mars's competitors just yet.

The Threat from Local Competitors

During the first twenty-five years of China's chocolate war, though plagued by the bane of copycats, the Big Five reigned virtually uncontested by any credible local competitors. However, an emerging trend that will be of increasing concern for these companies is the potential for local Chinese competitors to begin taking market share by employing tactics that have put multinational companies on the defensive in other consumer-product categories. Though local competitors remain a low-level threat even today, in the chocolate war of the future, the Big Five can no longer count on ineffectual local competition.

Though Mars was the first multinational company to begin producing chocolate to international standards in China, it wasn't the first company to do so. That distinction goes to local chocolate maker Le Conte,[11] which claims to have been the first to produce European-quality milk chocolate in China, when its factory in Shenzhen opened in 1990, three years before Mars started production. Le Conte was formed by the Chinese state-owned company COFCO, the country's largest agricultural company and food producer.[12] To establish its legitimacy as a maker of chocolate, which consumers perceived as a distinctly foreign product, the new company used the foreign-language brand Le Conte. As Chinese, Le Conte's business executives understood firsthand the foreign and exotic mystique surrounding chocolate, and they made the pitch to consumers that its products brought the "romantic aroma of the European continent to China." And, recognizing consumers' unusually deep emotional involvement with their chocolate, they employed the slogan, "Le Conte chocolate, only for your loved ones," a clearly emotional appeal.

At first, Le Conte faced only light competition from the Big Five, at that time all high-priced imports, and with COFCO aiding in national distribution of its chocolate bars, Le Conte enjoyed several years of high sales growth. But as Mars, and then Cadbury, Nestlé, and Hershey, began to enter the market, the novelty of these foreign brands pushed Le Conte to the sidelines. By the end of the 1990s, Le Conte's general manager, Lincoln Yuan, concluded that further competition with the multinationals was futile. Buyout discussions with Hershey began in 1999. The question for Hershey was whether acquiring Le Conte would be a quick and inexpensive way to get the company into in-country manufacturing—not a priority under Hershey's "build the business first, then build the infrastructure" model, but perhaps worth considering. However, after a preliminary fact-finding meeting, Yuan was gone and his successor quickly reversed course. The company was no longer seeking a buyer and was eager to give the Big Five a run for their money in China. This can-do spirit and self-confidence was emblematic of the shift in the mind-set of the Chinese people that marked the beginning of the "break-away phase" of China's transformational era after 2000. Far from the traditional Chinese copycat model, which is to make a quick buck off the fame of multinational brands, Le Conte was determined to win against the Big Five in the mainstream chocolate war. It is this mind-set that will ulti-mately lead to local competitors' becoming more of a threat to the Big Five in the future.

* * * * *

The first step in Le Conte's renewed efforts to compete with the multinationals was to hire a retired Rowntree[13] chocolate maker to come to China for three years to improve product quality. Chinese companies rarely pay the kind of money re-quired for outside consultants and advisers, so this was a strong indicator of Le Conte's determination. Product devel-opment and innovation also became high priorities.

The first few years of the new millennium saw Le Conte launch a surprisingly varied range of chocolate products, in-cluding aerated bars, bite-size chocolates in clear plastic boxes, and chocolates packaged in decorative tins and high-quality paper bags and boxes. It licensed images of Disney characters for the packaging of a new chocolate line targeting younger consumers. It created an entirely new range of chocolate-coated toasted oat, wheat, and rice clusters in plas-tic containers with pop-tops. Le Conte was rolling out new products with remarkable speed, often to match new products from competitors. For example, in the same season Mars launched a hazelnut cream-filled tubular wafer enrobed in chocolate, Le Conte began making a virtually identical product and got it to market in the same season. Though not all of its new products have survived the test of time, and as haphazard and unfocused as Le Conte appeared to be at times, its aggressive product-development efforts were further evidence of its determination to compete with the Big Five.

The company also met the multinationals head-on when it came to marketing. It heavily invested in in-store promotion and displays and made a significant investment in television advertising. Le Conte was not only determined to stay in the chocolate game, it was prepared to play the game on the level of its multinational competitors. But is it possible for Le Conte, with its little-engine-that-could determination, to threaten the dominance of the global chocolate players in China? It happened in Russia, during that country's transition to a market economy, when a company called Red October was largely abandoned by consumers for foreign brands after 1991 only to resurrect its brand five years later and take back the lead from its foreign rivals. But Russia was a country with a chocolate tradition dating to the 1880s and Russians had a long and nostalgic relationship with Red October that proved hard for the multinationals to dislodge. Le Conte didn't enjoy that kind of historic and emotional connection with Chinese consumers. Nevertheless, a love affair with all things foreign is just that—an affair—and it is possible that Chinese consumers could yet shift their still-shallow brand loyalty away from leading foreign brands like Dove and to a homegrown chocolate maker. The main reason for doing so would be price.

Le Conte's strategy is to strike at the Achilles' heel of the multinational companies: higher operating costs and resulting higher retail prices. It plans to win market share, and perhaps market leadership, by offering greater value to consumers. During the first kilometer of China's chocolate race, the market remained polarized between the high-priced, high-quality multinational brands and the low-quality, low-cost local products. Despite a three-to-one price differential, the majority of consumers have not budged from their unyielding support of the global brands. Le Conte believes, however, that if it can match the multinational brands in quality and taste with a 25 to 30 percent lower price, it can establish a value-for-money middle ground in the market that will draw consumers in from both the top and the bottom ends of the market, and with this strategy they might just win the war in the long run.

However, the company had learned a hard lesson during the early 2000s, when it directly engaged the Big Five in battle for market leadership in first-tier cities, substantially draining company coffers without succeeding with a middle-ground pricing strategy. Therefore, rather than compete where it is most expensive and competitive, in China's first-tier cities, the company recently shifted its business development focus to rapidly growing second-tier cities, where consumers are more price sensitive. Le Conte's strategy is not unlike the military strategy Mao used to lead Communist forces to power in China's thirty-three-year civil war that ended in 1950.

Mao's strategy, *Nong cun bao wei cheng shi*, or "rural encircling urban," was to avoid attacking the Chinese Nationalists in the country's major cities, their stronghold, and to dominate the rural areas where the Nationalists were weak. By doing so, Mao's army gained strength by acquiring resources and the popular support of China's vast peasant class, while effectively encircling Nationalist forces and confining them to the major cities. Mao's army eventually grew to an overwhelming force that captured the major cities and won the war. This strategy is now beginning to have an impact in other food and beverage categories with such Chinese companies as Wahaha[14] and its brand *feichang kele*, with the English name Future Cola (not a translation). Future Cola, born in 1998 and raised in the Chinese countryside, is now the country's third largest brand, and Wahaha has recently begun to take the cola war to Coke and Pepsi in China's big cities. But can Mao's "rural encircling urban" strategy work in China's chocolate war?

Thus far, the answer seems to be no. First, lower-tier cities and rural areas lack the air-conditioned distribution and retail infrastructure needed. The same infrastructure challenges that have hindered the Big Five from making inroads outside of the major cities have challenged Le Conte as well. Second, so far, purchasing patterns in lower-tier cities have not indicated that consumers are ready to adopt chocolate in significant numbers, their palates remaining literally ten to fifteen years behind those of consumers in the first-tier cities. Finally, significantly lower disposable incomes in lower-tier cities further limit chocolate's achievable potential there. Therefore, local chocolate companies like Le Conte have been unable to exploit the "rural encircling urban" strategy to any great effect.

Ironically, the most limiting factors for the Big Five chocolate companies in China—the need for an air-conditioned supply chain, untrained palates, and low incomes—have prevented local competition from making inroads using the "rural encircling urban" strategy. However, though these factors have made the Big Five resistant to local competition in the past, it would be perilous to assume that they have made them immune to it in the future, since all things in China are rapidly changing.

* * * * *

China's distribution infrastructure and quality retail environments continue to extend ever farther into China's second- and even third-tier cities, with enormous progress having been made within just the past few years. With each new air-conditioned hypermarket (superstore) or supermarket that opens in these locations, tens of thousands of people suddenly have access to chocolate for the first time. As this market expansion continues, even if 20 million of China's near billion inaccessible consumers emerge each year to become accessible consumers, it will take another half century for all of China's citizens to make this passage.

To reach these waves of new consumers, and to stay ahead of aggressive local competitors like Le Conte, the Big Five chocolate companies must push their products ever farther and deeper into China's emerging retail stores in second- and third-tier cities, using the same store-driven approach as they used successfully in the first-tier cities. However, given the geographic reach of these new markets, which number in the hundreds, the challenge will be significantly more complex. And it is this trend, continually unfolding over the coming decades, that defines China as a multitier market: one nation with people at distinctly different stages of development.

Managing China's Multitier Market Going Forward

To survive and prosper in China's multitier markets of the future, the Big Five chocolate companies will need to fight on two fronts. They will need to sustain their businesses in first-tier cities, while investing resources, both human and financial, in emerging second-tier cities. Failure to continue to push in the first-tier cities could mean ceding ground to multinational rivals. Failure to push into the lower-tier cities would mean conceding those markets to local competitors such as Le Conte. Striking the right balance between the competing priorities of current and future opportunities is the crux of any successful multitier market strategy, but this is the tightrope that each of the Big Five will have to walk to be successful in China for decades to come.

Past experience in China's first-tier cities will not necessarily be a roadmap for success in lower-tier cities for the Big Five, but some of the capabilities developed during the first two decades in China can be brought to bear. For example, no longer will the Big Five need to develop and build their entire local management talent from scratch; there is now a pool of experienced managers to deploy throughout the country.

The openness of mass communication, including the Internet, now used by more than 300 million Chinese, will also change the lower-tier market battlefield. Today, nationally broadcast television shows give Chinese in even the most remote locations a good look at the modern Chinese lifestyle in cities such as Beijing and Shanghai, whetting their appetites for all manner of goods, including chocolate. Though this will serve to accelerate development of chocolate consumers in lower-tier cities, the battle for these first-time consumers will, in some fundamental respects, be the same. Most significantly, it will still involve introducing an exotic and foreign curiosity to people whose palates are not accustomed to foreign tastes and textures.

To succeed in China's multitier market, the Big Five will need to understand and exploit their competitive advantages, which include their foreign heritage, product superiority, and management depth, and be realistic about their inherent limitations versus local competitors. Clearly their biggest strength is the credibility that foreign brands have with China's consumers—something local competitors cannot copy. But it can be lost. Nestlé lost much of its credibility in the chocolate category when it walked away from the high end of the market and pursued a series of lower-priced compound chocolates.

Product superiority has been another competitive advantage for the multinationals. Lacking extensive chocolate expertise, local companies must either copy or attempt to out-innovate the companies that have been working with chocolate for decades, and in some cases for more than a century. For example, Mars's Ethel M boxed chocolates—top-quality truffles and cream-filled boxed chocolates—became a success in China within one or two seasons but had years of product development in the American market behind it.

Further, China's multitier economy will demand some degree of product stratification: different products at different price ranges that meet the needs of distinctly different consumers at various stages of development. Companies such as Mars, which offers a wide range of products, are best positioned to compete across China's multitier markets. For example, with products ranging from RMB 2.5 ($0.37) for a snack-size Snickers bar to premium gift boxes approaching RMB 200 ($30), Mars can meet the needs of China's multitier market through selectively distributing its products according to consumers' level of development—that is, selling smaller Dove chocolate bars as an introductory offering for emerging consumers in second-tier cities, and high-priced Dove truffles and cream-filled boxed chocolates in cities with more sophisticated consumers, like Shanghai. However, effectively executing this for a country the size of China will require an extensive amount of coordination. Companies will need to build their business plans—in many cases, city by city—based on a complex decision matrix that includes factors such as geographic location, level of infrastructure development (e.g., number of air-conditioned stores), strength of the local distributors, level of general economic development (e.g., per capita income of local residents), and consumers' stage of chocolate development. Furthermore, this will be a dynamic process, since companies will need to continually reassess their priorities as millions of consumers simultaneously migrate through China's multitier market each year.

The Big Five chocolate companies generally have more management depth as well, particularly in marketing and the science behind effective retailing. They can, therefore, better capitalize on the rapid growth of modern retail stores in China, which, besides offering more air-conditioned points of distribution to fill with chocolate, enables them to leverage their extensive global retail experience. In doing so, they can effectively position themselves at the leading edge of China's retail revolution by introducing global retail best practices that are still new in China, such as the latest impulse merchandising techniques and category management.[15]

However, the Big Five need to consider their limitations in China, too. It is unrealistic for multinational companies, with their higher operating costs, to compete with local companies on price. Multinational companies generally employ at least some expatriate staff (a significant expense) and pay higher wages and benefits than do local companies. Most multinational subsidiaries also pay a kind of "internal tax" to their parent company to offset their share of the cost of regional management offices (e.g., an Asia Pacific office that oversees operations across multiple countries within the region) and even R&D costs at the head office. In addition, many foreign-invested companies in China are at a disadvantage when locally procuring commodities like milk and sugar, since local companies often receive more favorable pricing, particularly from state-owned companies. Therefore, with a higher built-in cost of operation, multinational companies that attempt to compete with local companies on price only jeopardize their sustainability through loss of long-term profitability. To credibly compete in the higher end of the market, foreign chocolate companies must continue to embrace their foreign heritage and jealously guard this unique competitive advantage.

Though China's chocolate market of the future will present new and daunting challenges, with tens of millions of new consumers becoming available each year, the Big Five will have more opportunity than ever to build a sustainable and profitable China business. And for all of its complexity, winning the future battles in China's chocolate war will demand precisely what it required in the past: the will to sustain a long-term commitment to the market, the stamina to see it through, and an unrelenting focus on meeting the expectations of China's emerging consumers.

* * * * *

During the 1998–1999 chocolate season, a Chinese husband and wife were shopping in a Shanghai hypermarket. The husband pushed the cart while the wife selected groceries. When they entered the chocolate aisle, the wife chose a chocolate and placed it in the cart. As she strolled to another aisle, the husband picked up the chocolate, looked it over front to back, and stiffened when he saw the price tag. Back on the shelf it went. When the wife returned and noticed the chocolate missing, she turned sharply and looked daggers at her husband. It didn't take but a second for the husband to realize that he had just made a big mistake, and he timidly put the chocolate back in the cart.

Clearly, at least some Chinese consumers have begun to make the same deep emotional connection with chocolate as have people around the world for millennia. Never before has the centuries-old dream of selling a product to every person in China been more within reach, and it is the prospect that humanity's passion for chocolate will spread to the remaining billion Chinese consumers in the coming decades that makes the chocolate war worth fighting.

Notes

Introduction—One Country, Three Centuries

1. Deng Xiaoping was a Chinese revolutionary and political figure who became China's paramount leader in 1978 and is credited with being the architect of China's current reform era.

2. Mao Zedong was a Chinese revolutionary, military, and political figure who rose to the position of Chairman of the People's Republic of China in 1954 and was the preeminent ruler of the country until his death in 1976.

Chapter 1—China and Chocolate: East Meets West

1. *Chanzu*, or foot binding, was a Chinese tradition of tightly binding a young girl's feet with bandages to deform them as they grew, breaking the toe bones and folding the toes back under the feet. This resulted in feet less than 6 inches in

length, something that men of the time found erotic. Painful and debilitating, the thousand-year-old practice was abolished with a government ban in 1911.

2. Confucius (551–479 BC) was a Chinese philosopher whose doctrines on morality, social relationships, justice, and sincerity are considered to have cast the principal social values upon which Chinese society was built.

3. A phrase attributed to Prime Minister Guan Zhong approximately 2,500 years ago.

4. Deng Xiaoping's reform era titles were Executive Vice Premier of the People's Republic of China (1975–1983), Chairman of the Chinese People's Political Consultative Conference (1978–1983), and Chairman of the Central Military Commission of the Chinese Communist Party (1981–1989). But he never was the formal head of state.

5. The thirteen-year period from 1937 to 1950, which included the Second Sino-Japanese War, which began in July 1937, and later became a part of World War II, which ended in 1945, followed by the 1946 collapse of a temporary truce in the on-going Chinese Civil War (1927–1950).

6. Many museums were deliberately burned and antiquities destroyed across the country during the Cultural Revolution.

7. Cross-docking is off-loading the cargo from one truck directly into another without the use of an intermediate facility such as a warehouse.

8. The ancient silk road consisted of a number of transcontinental land and sea trade routes that linked Asian and Mediterranean cultures through trade. Silk and other goods were transmitted along these routes, often passing through many hands in order to cross the Eurasian continent; China's official involvement began in earnest around 100 BC.

9. During the Cultural Revolution, universities were closed for years on end and millions of middle and high school students abandoned their classrooms to participate in this nationwide political movement. This generation is often referred

to as China's "lost generation," since few ever returned to school and consequently remained on the fringes of China's recent economic transformation. Furthermore, China's educational institutions were intellectually ransacked, with educators persecuted and imprisoned for long periods. China's education system took decades to recover.

10. Measured by national GDP. See World Development Indicators database, World Bank, September 10, 2008.

11. Kevin Hamlin, "China Property Slump Threatens Global Economy as Growth Slows," *Bloomberg News*, December 2, 2008.

12. Making solid milk chocolate required industrial machining technology for processing cocoa beans that did not exist until the nineteenth century. Also, cocoa beans contain a fat called cocoa butter. Since oil and water don't mix, and milk is largely water, early attempts at making milk chocolate with liquid milk resulted in an oily and milky mess. The advent of condensed milk and powdered milk during the second half of the 1800s solved this problem by removing water from the equation. Dark and white chocolate are also forms of milk chocolate, since they, too, contain milk solids.

13. According to a 1998 European Fair Trade Association report, Mars, Nestlé, Hershey, Cadbury, Ferrero, and Philip Morris (which owns Kraft-Jacobs-Suchard-Côte d'Or) accounted for about 80 percent of the global retail chocolate market.

14. Retail chocolate includes chocolate sold as candy in retail stores and excludes chocolate contained in foods such as cakes, cookies, and pastries.

15. In addition, China has eight major cuisine types: Shandong, Sichuan (Szechuan), Guangdong (Cantonese), Fujin, Jiangsu, Zhejiang, Hunan, and Anhui—all with their unique characteristics.

16. Chinese pharmacognosy is a dynamic system with new foods continually being evaluated and classified. Although it is unknown precisely when chocolate was classified as a food

that brings heat into the body, it is accepted among practitioners as being a heating food.

17. Coincidentally, it is not uncommon for Western doctors to suggest eating chocolate to reduce the discomfort of menstruation, and it is widely accepted in the West that chocolate is a cause of acne.

18. Within the doctrine of Chinese pharmacognosy there is no direct link between hot and cold weather and the body's internal "heat" and "cool" balance. This is a common misunderstanding.

19. Chocolate sales dropped off during summer months owing mainly to a contraction of distribution to air-conditioned stores and a hiatus in gift-giving holidays and events. However, per capita consumption of chocolate did dramatically decline during warm weather months too, due in large part to the belief that it is a "heaty" food.

20. It is estimated that the One Child Policy prevented 300 million births during its first twenty years.

21. Clay Chandler, "Little Emperors," *Fortune*, October 4, 2004.

22. The vast majority of China's population does not have physical access to chocolate and needs to be ruled out in order to arrive at a reasonable average chocolate consumption estimate among actual chocolate consumers.

23. Scantrack is a retail sales and marketing service that gathers information whenever consumers hear that "blip" at the checkout scanner in retail stores. This information is sold to manufacturers in weekly reports and allows them to monitor their products' performance and even product-category trends in stores.

24. Most stores in China were not willing to share their sales data with manufacturers, as they do in the United States and other developed markets.

25. Display racks within the checkout lane are referred to in the industry as being within the "arc of the reach" of consumers—roughly the 1-yard radius around the shopper.

26. In the United States during the first half of the twentieth century, confectioners had to go to great lengths to deal with the absence of air-conditioning. For example, in the summer months during the 1920s, the Peter Paul Candy Manufacturing Company made its Konabar—chocolate combined with coconut, fruits, and nuts—only at night and sold it door-to-door in its hometown of New Haven, Connecticut, early the next morning.

27. Business planning is typically based on the calendar year, but the chocolate peak season in China ran from August through April. To provide an overall picture of what happened during a single chocolate season, this book follows chocolate's seasonal year, which starts in July and completes in June of the following year—for example, the 2007–2008 chocolate season.

28. High-interest industries were strategic industries such as telecommunications, petroleum, and transportation. They were subject to extensive Chinese government involvement and oversight. Foreign car makers were required to form minority-ownership joint ventures with Chinese state-owned enterprises. While joint ventures offer certain advantages, such as a built-in government relationship, their success largely depended on the ability of the two parties to establish an effective working relationship. With the notorious lack of transparency of Chinese state-owned enterprises, joint ventures often amounted to an arranged wedding, where the groom would be allowed to lift the bridal veil on the wedding night.

Chapter 2—Ferrero Rocher: Accidental Hero

1. In the United States, KitKat is sold under license to Hershey.

2. A mooncake is a small, round, ruffled-edged cake with an

egg yolk in the center that looks like the moon when the cake is sliced in half.

3. An in-store promoter's job is to intercept shoppers in retail store aisles, introduce the products the store is promoting, and hand out free samples.

4. SKU is the acronym for stock-keeping unit, a term referring to a distinct item for sale.

5. "Jinsha" has no particular meaning and is a combination of the Chinese character *jin*, the metal gold, with the character *sha*, which when used in this context is a neutral character used to smoothly finish names of people or locations.

6. Associated Press, "China Tourists Stock Up on Infant Formula," *USA Today* online, March 5, 2004, www.usatoday .com/news/world/2004-05-03-hong-kong-formula_x.htm.

7. The Ferrero Rocher three-pack sells at over double the retail price of a Dove bar on a price-per-gram basis.

Chapter 3—Cadbury: One Billion Consumers

1. Chinese government census, which reported a population of 1.14 billion people in 1990.

2. Cadbury began making chocolate and cocoa beverages in 1831 but did not make solid milk chocolate for eating until 1897. Since Daniel Peters of Switzerland brought the first milk chocolate bar to market in 1875, twenty-two years before Cadbury, his company was first. Nestlé began marketing chocolate outside of its home country of Switzerland in 1904. The chocolate was produced by Daniel Peter's company Société Générale Suisse de Chocolat, and was sold under the Nestlé brand name. Nestlé eventually bought Peter's company in 1929. Therefore, through acquisition, Nestlé was the first of the Big Five chocolate companies to be in the solid milk chocolate business.

3. Harbin's weather is heavily influenced by Russia's Siberia region.

4. As a rule, automated packing equipment will pack chocolate bars at the same rate of speed, irrespective of size. Therefore, a production run of small chocolate bars will pack less chocolate in the same amount of time as a production run of big chocolate bars.

5. Éclairs were packaged similar to White Rabbit brand chewy milk candy, which had been a favorite of Chinese people since the mid-1940s.

6. Giving sweets as gifts to wedding banquet guests is a long-time Chinese tradition.

7. Cadbury press release, statement on the withdrawal of Cadbury chocolate, October 6, 2008.

Chapter 4—Hershey: Back to Basics

1. Designated the World's Columbian Exposition.

2. Millions of Filipinos work for extended periods outside of their home country each year to access higher-paying jobs in places like Hong Kong and Saudi Arabia.

3. Le Conte was owned and operated by a Chinese state-owned company.

4. Hershey manufactures many Cadbury brands under license for the U.S. market.

5. Ferrero did not switch to SIMS as its distributor until 2001.

6. Hershey's chocolates in China were labeled "Hershey's Extra Creamy Chocolate."

7. Dove is Mars's lead chocolate brand in China.

8. Shanghai led the nation in the number of convenience stores, which were nearly all air-conditioned.

9. Cadbury's packaging was purple, Nestlé's was red, and Mars's was chocolate brown.

10. China has one time zone, which is twelve hours ahead of Hershey, Pennsylvania's; therefore, e-mails from the head office would typically accumulate overnight in China.

11. One of the most common reasons that Chinese employees give for wanting to leave their companies is unfavorable and chaotic management changes.

12. Representative offices do pay tax in China, based on a percentage of their operating expenses. However, this is typically far below what the taxes would be for a commercial operation of the same size.

13. WFOE is an acronym for Wholly Foreign-Owned Enterprise, which is a legal entity created in China exclusively by a foreign entity.

Chapter 5—Nestlé: China's Chocolate War Sideshow

1. Nestlé also markets nonfood products through one of its acquisitions, Alcon, and through a company in which it has an equity interest, L'Oréal.

2. *Nestlé* means "small bird's nest" in his ancestor's regional German dialect.

3. Conversion method: based on the relative values of the two currencies to gold in 1874, and application of the Consumer Price Index method to calculate equivalent 2007 U.S. dollar value.

4. This company merged with Nestlé in 1905. Indeed, from 1905 to 1947 the company was known as Nestlé and Anglo-Swiss Condensed Milk Company. It changed its name to Nestlé Alimentana S.A. in 1947 and began using its current name, Nestlé S.A., in 1977.

5. Dannon is the company's brand name in the United States.

6. Incorporated as Nestlé (China) Investment Services, later simplified to Nestlé (China), Ltd.

7. Nestlé (China), Ltd. was not used as a holding company, since the manufacturing companies were incorporations of Nestlé S.A. of Switzerland and operated under separate provincial-level business licenses.

8. Nestlé had 232,000 employees worldwide in 1998. Source: Nestlé S.A. 2008 Annual Report.

9. Excludes the brief tenure of a Nestlé China market head in 1995, who was moved to Japan to fill an urgent vacancy.

10. Wafer is far less dense than chocolate and the result was a much larger bar than one made of solid chocolate of a similar weight.

11. Though equipment was available at the Tianjin factory to produce the Nestlé Wafer, it was small scale and incapable of supplying enough product to support a national launch.

12. The Nestlé China logo is a combination of Nestlé's Chinese brand QueQiao (which means bird's nest), followed by the foreign-language Nestlé brand.

13. Under Nestlé China's unified packaging, the KitKat logo was located below the Nestlé China logo and was the smaller of the two. The logo size ratio guidelines for China-made Kit-Kat were the Nestlé master brand logo 70 percent and the KitKat subbrand 30 percent. This made the KitKat logo very difficult to see from a distance at first glance.

14. The new molded chocolate bars were still required to follow Nestlé's unified branding and packaging guidelines but were given more latitude. They employed an enhanced logo and used a more premium foil wrapper.

15. Nescafé did find a following among China's taxi drivers, who valued the Nescafé and CoffeeMate jars because they could hold a large volume of tea, be handily resealed with their screw-top lid to prevent spilling, and fit snugly between the two front seats of their taxis. They were also handy spittoons, for the same reasons.

Chapter 6—Mars: A Well-Regulated Militia

1. According to Sinomonitor International, a Sino-Japanese independent marketing monitoring company established in 1997. This is based on a 2004 China Marketing and Media Study (CMMS) survey, which followed over 70,000 Chinese consumers between the ages of fifteen and sixty-four, in thirty major cities.

2. Mars refers to its employees as "associates." The figure included both chocolate and pet-food businesses.

3. Enrobing is a production-line chocolate-dipping process whereby the chocolate is layered onto one or a combination of ingredients.

4. Milky Way outside of the United States does not contain caramel.

5. The 3 Musketeers bar is marketed under the Milky Way brand outside the United States. M&Ms candy-coated chocolate, the chocolate that "melts in your mouth, not in your hand," conveniently addressed chocolate's main distribution challenge of the time: lack of a well-developed air-conditioned supply chain. The name comes from the first letter of the names Mars and Murrie. Forrest Mars had taken a business partner named Bruce Murrie at the time M&Ms were developed.

6. "The World's Billionaires," *Forbes.com*, March 5, 2008.

7. Some local chocolate companies did manage to maintain a presence in the market, though they were a very small component of the total market and constituted little if any competitive threat to internationally branded players at the time. They mainly served as a bottom for the market, for local players did not have the quality or credibility to compete in the mainstream chocolate market.

8. Even though he was fast approaching the age of eighty, Forrest Mars Sr. started a premium-boxed-chocolate business

in 1981 named Ethel M Chocolates, a tribute to his mother, and he ran it as a separate company until Mars Inc. bought the company in 1988.

9. This was a lesson the company may have learned in Russia. Mars and other Western chocolate brands made a bad first impression with Russian consumers after 1991, since smugglers and street vendors mishandled the product, resulting in heat-damaged goods being widely sold to consumers.

10. Pic'n'mix is a retail display composed of bulk bins containing small pack-sizes of various products that are clustered together. Consumers are allowed to pick and mix the various products, which are typically sold by weight. In modern-trade retail stores, they were typically limited to one location in the store, usually at the back of the food section, and contained a number of companies' products.

11. John Mars is the current chairman of the company, Forrest Mars Jr. was CEO (retired), and as of 2004 Jacqueline Mars was vice president.

12. Steven N. Kaplan and Bernadette A. Minton, "How Has CEO Turnover Changed?" (Chicago: University of Chicago Graduate School of Business, 2006), http://faculty.chicagobooth.edu/steven.kaplan/research/km.pdf. This study of CEO turnover rates at publicly traded Fortune 500 companies cites 16.45 percent between 1998 and 2005, which implies an average CEO turnover of just over six years.

Chapter 7—Going the Distance: China's 10K Chocolate Race

1. *The 2008 World Factbook* (United States Central Intelligence Agency, March 5, 2009, edition), available at https://www.cia.gov/library/publications/the-world-factbook/index.html. GDP ranking was determined by comparing estimated 2008 GDP (at official exchange rates) shown in the individual country

listings of the United States at US$14.3 trillion, Japan at US$4.8 trillion, China at US$4.2 trillion, and Germany at US$3.8 trillion.

2. According to a Euromonitor 2004 estimate, global retail chocolate sales were US$65 billion.

3. The official name is the Wenchuan earthquake, named for the region near the epicenter.

4. China's Xinhua News Agency, January 22, 2009.

5. Commercial users of milk around the world regularly test protein levels in the milk they purchase. One common test measures for the presence of nitrogen, an indicator of protein levels. Some individual farmers and milk collection wholesalers in China systematically added melamine to their milk, since its nitrogen content created false high-protein readings in low-protein or watered-down milk. Melamine causes a variety of kidney ailments—including kidney stones—some of which can be fatal. Once in China's milk supply, melamine contamination spread to other products that use milk, including chocolate, infant formula, dairy-based coffee creamer, ice cream, cookies, and candies.

6. Imported Hershey products, primarily Hershey's Kisses, began to reappear on shelves during the 2005–2006 chocolate season, but only in small volumes and in a limited number of stores.

7. A recent spate of high-profile incidents within the region involving pesticide and parasite contamination of Chinese vegetables, poultry, and packaged foods has only added to concerns about the safety and purity of made-in-China food products.

8. Excluding Canada and Mexico, where Hershey has had successful businesses for decades.

9. Hershey's 2007 net sales outside of the United States were 13.8 percent of total company sales. Hershey now defines its business in two segments: the "Americas," which includes the United States, Canada, Mexico, and Brazil, and "Other

International," which is composed of all other international operations. Hershey's Americas business accounted for over 90 percent of total company sales in 2007, with Other International accounting for less than 10 percent. Source: The Hershey Company 2007 Annual Report.

10. Mars (Jiaxing) Incorporated is a $90 million wholly foreign-invested project by Mars Incorporated.

11. Incorporated as Shenzhen Le Conte Food Co., Ltd., in 1990. The Chinese brand name is *Jindi*, which combines the Chinese characters *Jin*, meaning "gold," and *Di*, which is the second character in the combination of characters *Huangdi*, meaning "emperor."

12. COFCO is an acronym for China National Cereals, Oils & Foodstuffs Corporation. It incorporated Le Conte with a minority investor, a mysterious British Virgin Island company known only as BVI No. 102, which has a 14 percent stake in Le Conte.

13. Rowntree & Company is a British chocolate company acquired by Nestlé in 1988.

14. Wahaha Group Company Ltd. was founded as a government-owned company in 1987, in Hangzhou, China. Twenty years later, Wahaha has become China's largest domestic beverage company, reporting 2007 total sales revenue of approximately RMB 25.8 billion (US$3.8 billion). The company's main products are bottled water, milk drinks, tea drinks, and carbonated beverages, which have been predominantly sold in the country's lower-tier cities and rural areas.

15. Category management is a well-established practice in larger retail stores in developed economies. Product categories, such as chocolate, are managed as individual business units within stores. Retailers often call upon a supplier (usually the market leader) to manage all the brands within the category on behalf of the retailer. The idea is to allow chocolate industry experts, with their in-depth industry knowledge, to maximize sales of the category for retailers.

Index